J. S. Mill's Logic (1843)
Principles of Political Economy (1848)
Autobiography modified (1879)

OTHER BOOKS BY BERTRAND RUSSELL
AVAILABLE IN CLARION EDITION

The Basic Writings of Bertrand Russell
A History of Western Philosophy
Human Knowledge: Its Scope and Limits
Philosophical Essays
Unpopular Essays
Why I Am Not a Christian

PORTRAITS FROM MEMORY

and Other Essays
by

BERTRAND RUSSELL

A CLARION BOOK
PUBLISHED BY SIMON AND SCHUSTER

A Clarion Book
Published by Simon and Schuster
Rockefeller Center, 630 Fifth Avenue
New York, New York 10020
All rights reserved
including the right of reproduction
in whole or in part in any form
Copyright © 1951, 1952, 1953, 1956 by Bertrand Russell

Second paperback printing, 1969

SBN 671-20378-9
Library of Congress Catalog Card Number: 56-11187
Manufactured in the United States of America

CONTENTS

	PAGE
Adaptation: an Autobiographical Epitome	1
Six Autobiographical Essays:	13
I. Why I Took to Philosophy	13
II. Some Philosophical Contacts	19
III. Experiences of a Pacifist in the First World War	26
IV. From Logic to Politics	32
V. Beliefs: Discarded and Retained	38
VI. Hopes: Realized and Disappointed	44
How to Grow Old	50
Reflections on My Eightieth Birthday	54
Portraits from Memory	60
I. Some Cambridge Dons of the Nineties	60
II. Some of My Contemporaries at Cambridge	67
III. George Bernard Shaw	75
IV. H. G. Wells	81
V. Joseph Conrad	86
VI. George Santayana	92
VII. Alfred North Whitehead	99
VIII. Sidney and Beatrice Webb	105
IX. D. H. Lawrence	111
Lord John Russell	117
John Stuart Mill	122

v

	PAGE
Mind and Matter	145
The Cult of "Common Usage"	166
Knowledge and Wisdom	173
A Philosophy for Our Time	178
A Plea for Clear Thinking	185
History as an Art	190
How I Write	210
The Road to Happiness	215
Symptoms of Orwell's 1984	221
Why I Am Not a Communist	229
Man's Peril	233
Steps Toward Peace	239

Adaptation:

An Autobiographical Epitome

For those who are too young to remember the world before 1914, it must be difficult to imagine the contrast for a man of my age between childhood memories and the world of the present day. I try, though with indifferent success, to accustom myself to a world of crumbling empires, Communism, atom bombs, Asian self-assertion, and aristocratic downfall. In this strange insecure world where no one knows whether he will be alive tomorrow, and where ancient states vanish like morning mists, it is not easy for those who, in youth, were accustomed to ancient solidities to believe that what they are now experiencing is a reality and not a transient nightmare. Very little remains of institutions and ways of life that when I was a child appeared as indestructible as granite. I grew up in an atmosphere impregnated with tradition. My parents died before I can remember, and I was brought up by my grandparents. My grandfather was born in the early days of the French Revolution and was in Parliament while Napoleon was still Emperor. As a Whig who followed Fox, he thought the English hostility to the French Revolution and Napoleon excessive, and he visited the exiled Emperor in Elba. It was he who, in 1832, introduced the Reform Bill which started England on the road toward democracy. He was Prime Minister during the Mexican War and during the revolutions of 1848. In common with the whole Russell family, he inherited the peculiar brand of aristocratic liberalism which characterized the Revolution of 1688 in which his ancestor played an important part. I was taught a kind of theoretic republicanism which was prepared to tolerate a monarch so long as he recognized that he was an employee of the people and subject to dismissal if he proved unsatisfactory. My grandfather, who was no respecter of persons, used to explain this point of view to Queen Victoria, and she was not altogether sympathetic. She did, however, give him the house in Richmond Park in which I spent all my youth. I imbibed certain political principles and expectations, and have on the whole retained the former in spite of being compelled to reject the latter. There was to be ordered progress throughout the world, no revolutions, a gradual cessation of war, and an extension of parliamentary government to all those unfortunate regions which did not yet enjoy it. My grandmother used to laugh about a conversation she had had with the Russian Ambassador. She said to him, "Perhaps some day you will have a parliament in Russia," and he replied, "God forbid, my dear Lady John." The Russian Ambassador of today might give the same answer if he changed the first word. The hopes of that period seem now a little absurd. There was to be democracy, but it was assumed that the people would always be ready to follow the advice of wise and experienced aristocrats. There was to be a disappearance of imperialism, but the subject races in Asia and Africa, whom the British would voluntarily cease to govern, would have learned the advantage of a bicameral legislature composed of Whigs and Tories in about equal numbers, and would reproduce in torrid zones the parliamentary duels of Disraeli and Gladstone which were at their most brilliant at the time when I imbibed my dominant political prejudices. The idea of any insecurity to British power never entered anybody's head. Britannia ruled the waves, and that was that. There was, it is true, Bismarck, whom I was taught to consider a rascal; but it was thought that the civilizing influences of Goethe and Schiller would prevent the Germans from being permanently led into wrong paths by this uncivilized farmer. It was true also that there had been violence in the not-so-distant past. The French in their Revolution had committed excesses which one must deplore, while urging, at the same time, that reactionaries had grossly exaggerated them and that they would not have occurred at all but for the foolish hostility of the rest of Europe to progressive opinions in France. It might perhaps be admitted also that Cromwell had gone too far in cutting off the king's head but, broadly speaking, anything done against kings was to be applauded—unless, indeed, it were done by priests, like Becket, in which case one sided with the king. The atmosphere in the house was one of puritan piety and austerity. There were family prayers at eight o'clock every morning. Although there were eight servants, food was always of Spartan simplicity, and even what there was, if it was at all nice, was considered too good for children. For instance, if there was apple tart and rice pudding, I was only allowed the rice pudding. Cold baths all the year round were insisted upon, and I had to practice the piano from seven-thirty to eight every morning although the fires were not yet lit. My grandmother never allowed herself to sit in an armchair until the evening. Alcohol and tobacco were viewed with disfavor although stern convention compelled them to serve a little wine to guests. Only virtue was prized, virtue at the expense of intellect, health, happiness, and every mundane good.

I rebelled against this atmosphere first in the name of intellect. I was a solitary, shy, priggish youth. I had no experience of the social pleasures of boyhood and did not miss them.

But I liked mathematics, and mathematics was suspect because it has no ethical content. I came also to disagree with the theological opinions of my family, and as I grew up I became increasingly interested in philosophy, of which they profoundly disapproved. Every time the subject came up they repeated with unfailing regularity, "What is mind? No matter. What is matter? Never mind." After some fifty or sixty repetitions, this remark ceased to amuse me.

When at the age of eighteen I went up to Cambridge, I found myself suddenly and almost bewilderingly among people who spoke the sort of language that was natural to me. If I said anything that I really thought they neither stared at me as if I were a lunatic nor denounced me as if I were a criminal. I had been compelled to live in a morbid atmosphere where an unwholesome kind of morality was encouraged to such an extent as to paralyze intelligence. And to find myself in a world where intelligence was valued and clear thinking was thought to be a good thing caused me an intoxicating delight. It is sometimes said that those who have had an unconventional education will find a difficulty in adjusting themselves to the world. I had no such experience. The environment in which I found myself at Cambridge fitted me like a glove. In the course of my first term I made lifelong friends and I never again had to endure the almost unbearable loneliness of my adolescent years. My first three years at Cambridge were given to mathematics and my fourth year to philosophy. I came in time to think ill of the philosophy that I had been taught, but the learning of it was a delight and it opened to me new and fascinating problems which I hoped to be able to solve. I was especially attracted to problems concerning the foundations of mathematics. I wished to believe that some knowledge is certain and I thought that the best hope of finding certain knowledge was in mathematics. At the same time it was obvious to me that the proofs of mathematical propositions which my teachers had offered me were fallacious. I hoped that better proofs were forthcoming. Subsequent study showed me that my hopes were partly justified. But it took me nearly twenty years to find all the justification that seemed possible and even that fell far short of my youthful hopes.

When I had finished my student years at Cambridge, I had to decide whether to devote my life to philosophy or to politics. Politics had been the habitual pursuit of my family since the sixteenth century, and to think of anything else was viewed as a kind of treachery to my ancestors. Everything was done to show that my path would be smooth if I chose politics. John Morley, who was Irish Secretary, offered me a post. Lord Dufferin, who was British Ambassador in Paris, gave me a job at our Embassy there. My family brought pressure to bear upon me in every way they could think of. For a time I hesitated, but in the end the lure of philosophy proved irresistible. This was my first experience of conflict, and I found it painful. I have since had so much conflict that many people have supposed that I must like it. I should, however, have much preferred to live at peace with everybody. But over and over again profound convictions have forced me into disagreements, even where I least desired them. After I had decided on philosophy, however, everything went smoothly for a long time. I lived mainly in an academic atmosphere where the pursuit of philosophy was not regarded as an eccentric folly. All went well until 1914. But when the First World War broke out, I thought it was a folly and a crime on the part of every one of the Powers involved on both sides. I hoped that England might remain neutral and, when this did not happen, I continued to protest. I found myself isolated from most of my former friends and, what I minded even

more, estranged from the current of the national life. I had
to fall back upon sources of strength that I hardly knew
myself to possess. But something, that if I had been religious
I should have called the Voice of God, compelled me to persist. Neither then nor later did I think *all* war wrong. It was
that war, not all war, that I condemned. The Second World
War I thought necessary, not because I had changed my opinions on war, but because the circumstances were different. In
fact all that made the Second War necessary was an outcome
of the First War. We owe to the First War and its aftermath
Russian Communism, Italian Fascism and German Nazism.
We owe to the First War the creation of a chaotic unstable
world where there is every reason to fear that the Second
World War was not the last, where there is the vast horror of
Russian Communism to be combatted, where Germany,
France and what used to be the Austro-Hungarian Empire
have all fallen lower in the scale of civilization, where there
is every prospect of chaos in Asia and Africa, where the
prospect of vast and horrible carnage inspires daily and
hourly terror. All these evils have sprung with the inevitabil-
ity of Greek tragedy out of the First World War. Consider
by way of contrast what would have happened if Britain had
remained neutral in that war. The war would have been
short. It would have ended in victory for Germany. America would not have been dragged in. Britain would have remained strong and prosperous. Germany would not have
been driven into Nazism; Russia, though it would have had a
revolution, would in all likelihood have not had the Communist Revolution, since it could not in a short war have been
reduced to the condition of utter chaos which prevailed in
1917. The Kaiser's Germany, although war propaganda on
our side represented it as atrocious, was in fact only swash-
buckling and a little absurd. I had lived in the Kaiser's Ger-

many and I knew that progressive forces in that country were very strong and had every prospect of ultimate success. There was more freedom in the Kaiser's Germany than there is now in any country outside Britain and Scandinavia. We were told at the time that it was a war for freedom, a war for democracy and a war against militarism. As a result of that war freedom has vastly diminished and militarism has vastly increased. As for democracy, its future is still in doubt. I cannot think that the world would now be in anything like the bad state in which it is if English neutrality in the First War had allowed a quick victory to Germany. On these grounds I have never thought that I was mistaken in the line that I took at that time. I also do not regret having attempted throughout the war years to persuade people that the Germans were less wicked than official propaganda represented them as being, for a great deal of the subsequent evil resulted from the severity of the Treaty of Versailles and this severity would not have been possible but for the moral horror with which Germany was viewed. The Second World War was a totally different matter. Very largely as a result of our follies, Nazi Germany had to be fought if human life was to remain tolerable. If the Russians seek world dominion it is to be feared that war with them will be supposed equally necessary. But all this dreadful sequence is an outcome of the mistakes of 1914 and would not have occurred if those mistakes had been avoided.

The end of the First War was not the end of my isolation, but, on the contrary, the prelude to an even more complete isolation (except from close personal friends) which was due to my failure to applaud the new revolutionary government of Russia. When the Russian Revolution first broke out I welcomed it as did almost everybody else, including the British Embassy in Petrograd (as it then was). It was difficult at a distance to follow the confused events of 1918 and 1919 and I did not know what to think of the Bolsheviks. But in 1920 I went to Russia, had long talks with Lenin and other prominent men, and saw as much as I could of what was going on. I came to the conclusion that everything that was being done and everything that was being intended was totally contrary to what any person of a liberal outlook would desire. I thought the regime already hateful and certain to become more so. I found the source of evil in a contempt for liberty and democracy which was a natural outcome of fanaticism. It was thought by radicals in those days that one ought to support the Russian Revolution whatever it might be doing, since it was opposed by reactionaries, and criticism of it played into their hands. I felt the force of this argument and was for some time in doubt as to what I ought to do. But in the end I decided in favor of what seemed to me to be the truth. I stated publicly that I thought the Bolshevik regime abominable, and I have never seen any reason to change this opinion. In this I differed from almost all the friends that I had acquired since 1914. Most people still hated me for having opposed the war, and the minority, who did not hate me on this ground, denounced me for not praising the Bolsheviks.

My visit to Russia in 1920 was a turning point in my life. During the time that I was there I felt a gradually increasing horror which became an almost intolerable oppression. The country seemed to me one vast prison in which the jailers were cruel bigots. When I found my friends applauding these men as liberators and regarding the regime that they were creating as a paradise, I wondered in a bewildered manner whether it was my friends or I that were mad. But the habit of following my own judgment rather than that of others had grown strong in me during the war years. And as a mat-

ter of historical dynamics it seemed obvious that revolutionary ardor must develop into imperialism as it had done in
the French Revolution. When I finally decided to say what
I thought of the Bolsheviks my former political friends, including very many who have since come to my opinion, denounced me as a lackey of the *bourgeoisie*. But reactionaries
did not notice what I said and continued to describe me in
print as a "lily-livered Bolshie swine." And so I succeeded in
getting the worst of both worlds.

All this would have been more painful than it was if I had
not, just at that moment, had occasion to go to China where
I spent a year in great happiness away from the European
turmoil. Since that time, although I have had occasional conflicts, they have been more external and less painful than those
connected with the war and the Bolsheviks.

After I returned from China in 1921 I became absorbed
for a number of years in parenthood and attendant problems
of education. I did not like conventional education but I
thought what is called "progressive education" in most
schools deficient on the purely scholastic side. It seemed to
me, and still seems, that in a technically complex civilization
such as ours a man cannot play an important part unless in
youth he has had a very considerable dose of sheer instruction. I could not find any school at that time that seemed to
me satisfactory, so I tried starting a school of my own. But
a school is an administrative enterprise and I found myself
deficient in skill as an administrator. The school, therefore,
was a failure. But fortunately about this time I found another
school which had recently become excellent. I wrote two
books on education and spent a lot of time thinking about it
but, as anyone might have expected, I was better at talking
than at doing. I am not a believer in complete freedom during childhood. I think children need a fixed routine, though

there should be days when it is not carried out. I think also that, if a person when adult is to be able to fit into a society, he must learn while still young that he is not the center of the universe and that his wishes are often not the most important factor in a situation. I think also that the encouragement of originality without technical skill, which is practiced in many progressive schools, is a mistake. There are some things that I like very much in progressive education, especially freedom of speech, and freedom to explore the facts of life, and the absence of a silly kind of morality which is more shocked by the utterance of a swear word than by an unkind action. But I think that those who have rebelled against an unwise discipline have often gone too far in forgetting that some discipline is necessary. This applies more especially to the acquisition of knowledge.

Age and experience have not had as much effect upon my opinions as no doubt they ought to have had, but I have come to realize that freedom is a principle to which there are very important limitations of which those in education are in a certain sense typical. What people will do in given circumstances depends enormously upon their habits; and good habits are not acquired without discipline. Most of us go through life without stealing, but many centuries of police discipline have gone into producing this abstention which now seems natural. If children are taught nothing about manners they will snatch each others' food and the older children will get all the titbits. In international affairs it will not be by prolonging interstate anarchy that the world will be brought back to a tolerable condition, but by the rule of international law, which will never prevail unless backed by international force. In the economic sphere the old doctrine of *laissez faire* is not now held by any practical men, although a few dreamers still hanker after it. As the world grows fuller, regulation becomes more necessary. No doubt this is regrettable. The world of the *Odyssey* is attractive. One sails from island to island and always finds a lovely lady ready to receive one. But nowadays immigration quotas interfere with this sort of life. It was all very well for Odysseus, who was only one, but if a hundred million Chinese had descended upon Calypso's island, life would have become rather difficult. The broad rule is a simple one: that men should be free in what only concerns themselves, but that they should not be free when they are tempted to aggression against others. But although the broad rule is simple, the carrying out of it in detail is very complex, and so the problem of the proper limitations on human freedom remains.

Although I have been much occupied with the world and the vast events that have taken place during my lifetime, I have always thought of myself as primarily an abstract philosopher. I have tried to extend the exact and demonstrative methods of mathematics and science into regions traditionally given over to vague speculation. I like precision. I like sharp outlines. I hate misty vagueness. For some reason which I do not profess to understand, this has caused large sections of the public to think of me as a cold person destitute of passion. It seems to be supposed that whoever feels any passion must enjoy self-deception and choose to live in a fool's paradise on the ground that no other sort of paradise is attainable. I cannot sympathize with this point of view. The more I am interested in anything, the more I wish to know the truth about it, however unpleasant the truth may be. When I first became interested in philosophy, I hoped that I should find in it some satisfaction for my thwarted desire for a religion. For a time, I found a sort of cold comfort in Plato's eternal world of ideas. But in the end I thought this was nonsense and I have found in philosophy no satisfaction whatever for the impulse toward religious belief. In this sense I have found philosophy disappointing, but as a clarifier I have found it quite the opposite. Many things which, when I was young, were matters of taste or conjecture have become exact and scientific. In this I rejoice and in so far as I have been able to contribute to the result I feel that my work in philosophy has been worth doing.

But in such a world as we now have to live in, it grows increasingly difficult to concentrate on abstract matters. The everyday world presses in upon the philosopher and his ivory tower begins to crumble. The future of mankind more and more absorbs my thoughts. I grew up in the full flood of Victorian optimism, and although the easy cheerfulness of that time is no longer possible, something remains with me of the hopefulness that then was easy. It is now no longer easy. It demands a certain fortitude and a certain capacity to look beyond the moment to a more distant future. But I remain convinced, whatever dark times may lie before us, that mankind will emerge, that the habit of mutual forbearance, which now seems lost, will be recovered, and that the reign of brutal violence will not last forever. Mankind has to learn some new lessons of which the necessity is due to increase of skill without increase of wisdom. Moral and intellectual requirements are inextricably intertwined. Evil passions make men incapable of seeing the truth, and false beliefs afford excuses for evil passions. If the world is to emerge, it requires both clear thinking and kindly feeling. It may be that neither will be learned except through utmost disaster. I hope this is not the case. I hope that something less painful can teach wisdom. But by whatever arduous road, I am convinced that the new wisdom which the new world requires will be learned sooner or later, and that the best part of human history lies in the future, not in the past.

Why I Took to Philosophy

THE motives which have led men to become philosophers have been of various kinds. The most respectable motive was the desire to understand the world. In early days, while philosophy and science were indistinguishable, this motive predominated. Another motive which was a potent incentive in early times was the illusoriness of the senses. Such questions as: Where is the rainbow? Are things really what they seem to be in sunshine or in moonlight? In more modern forms of the same problem—Are things really what they look like to the naked eye or what they look like through a microscope? Such puzzles, however, very soon came to be supplemented by a larger problem. When the Greeks began to be doubtful about the gods of Olympus, some of them sought in philosophy a substitute for traditional beliefs. Through the combination of these two motives there arose a twofold movement in philosophy: on the one hand, it was thought to show that much which passes for knowledge in everyday life is not real knowledge; and on the other hand, that there is a deeper philosophical truth which, according to most philosophers, is more consonant than our everyday beliefs with what we should wish the universe to be. In almost all philosophy doubt has been the goad and certainty has been the goal. There has been doubt about the senses, doubt about science, and doubt about theology. In some philosophers one of these has been more prominent, in others another. Philosophers have also differed widely as to the answers they have suggested to these doubts and even as to whether any answers are possible.

All the traditional motives combined to lead me to philosophy, but there were two that specially influenced me. The one which operated first and continued longest was the desire to find some knowledge that could be accepted as certainly true. The other motive was the desire to find some satisfaction for religious impulses.

I think the first thing that led me toward philosophy (though at that time the word "philosophy" was still unknown to me) occurred at the age of eleven. My childhood was mainly solitary as my only brother was seven years older than I was. No doubt as a result of much solitude I became rather solemn, with a great deal of time for thinking but not much knowledge for my thoughtfulness to exercise itself upon. I had, though I was not yet aware of it, the pleasure in demonstrations which is typical of the mathematical mind. After I grew up I found others who felt as I did on this matter. My friend G. H. Hardy, who was professor of pure mathematics, enjoyed this pleasure in a very high degree. He told me once that if he could find a proof that I was going to die in five minutes he would of course be sorry to lose me, but this sorrow would be quite outweighed by pleasure in the proof. I entirely sympathized with him and was not at all offended. Before I began the study of geometry somebody had told me that it proved things and this caused me to feel delight when my brother said he would teach it to me. Geometry in those days was still "Euclid." My brother began at the beginning with the definitions. These I accepted readily enough. But he came next to the axioms. "These," he said, "can't be proved, but they have to be assumed before the rest can be proved." At these words my hopes crumbled. I had thought it would be wonderful to find something that one could *prove*, and then it turned out that this could only be done by means of assumptions of which there was no proof. I looked at my brother with a sort of indignation and said: "But why should I admit these things if they can't be proved?" He replied, "Well, if you won't, we can't go on." I thought it might be worth while to learn the rest of the story, so I agreed to admit the axioms for the time being. But I remained full of doubt and perplexity as regards a region in which I had hoped to find indisputable clarity. In spite of these doubts, which at most times I forgot, and which I usually supposed capable of some answer not yet known to me, I found great delight in mathematics—much more delight, in fact, than in any other study. I liked to think of the applications of mathematics to the physical world, and I hoped that in time there would be a mathematics of human behavior as precise as the mathematics of machines. I hoped this because I liked demonstrations, and at most times this motive outweighed the desire, which I also felt, to believe in free will. Nevertheless I never quite overcame my fundamental doubts as to the validity of mathematics.

When I began to learn higher mathematics, fresh difficulties assailed me. My teachers offered me proofs which I felt to be fallacious and which, as I learned later, had been recognized as fallacious. I did not know then, or for some time after I had left Cambridge, that better proofs had been found by German mathematicians. I therefore remained in a receptive mood for the heroic measures of Kant's philosophy. This suggested a large new survey from which such difficulties as had troubled me looked niggling and unimportant. All this I came later on to think wholly fallacious, but that was only after I had allowed myself to sink deep in the mire of metaphysical muddles. I was encouraged in my transition to philosophy by a certain disgust with mathematics, resulting from too much concentration and too much absorption in the sort of skill that is needed in examinations. The attempt to acquire examination technique had led me to think of mathematics as consisting of artful dodges and ingenious devices and as altogether too much like a crossword puzzle. When, at the end of my first three years at Cambridge, I emerged from my last mathematical examination I swore that I would never look at mathematics again and sold all my mathematical books. In this mood the survey of philosophy gave me all the delight of a new landscape on emerging from a valley.

It had not been only in mathematics that I sought certainty. Like Descartes (whose work was still unknown to me) I thought that my own existence was, to me, indubitable. Like him, I felt it possible to suppose that the outer world is nothing but a dream. But even if it be, it is a dream that is really dreamed, and the fact that I experience it remains unshakably certain. This line of thought occurred to me first when I was sixteen, and I was glad when I learned later that Descartes had made it the basis of his philosophy.

At Cambridge my interest in philosophy received a stimulus from another motive. The skepticism which had led me to doubt even mathematics had also led me to question the fundamental dogmas of religion, but I ardently desired to find a way of preserving at least something that could be called religious belief. From the age of fifteen to the age of eighteen I spent a great deal of time and thought on religious belief. I examined fundamental dogmas one by one, hoping with all my heart to find some reason for accepting them. I wrote my thoughts in a notebook which I still possess. They were, of course, crude and youthful, but for the moment I saw no answer to the agnosticism which they suggested. At Cambridge I was made aware of whole systems of thought of which I had previously been ignorant and I abandoned for a time the ideas which I had worked out in solitude. At Cambridge I was introduced to the philosophy of Hegel who, in the course of nineteen abstruse volumes, professed to have proved something which would do quite well as an emended and sophisticated version of traditional beliefs. Hegel thought of the universe as a closely knit unity. His universe was like a jelly in the fact that, if you touched any one part of it, the whole quivered; but it was unlike a jelly in the fact that it could not really be cut up into parts. The appearance of consisting of parts, according to him, was a delusion. The only reality was the Absolute, which was his name for God. In this philosophy I found comfort for a time. As presented to me by its adherents, especially McTaggart, who was then an intimate friend of mine, Hegel's philosophy had seemed both charming and demonstrable. McTaggart was a philosopher some six years senior to me and throughout his life an ardent disciple of Hegel. He influenced his contemporaries very considerably, and I for a time fell under his sway. There was a curious pleasure in making oneself believe that time and space are unreal, that matter is an illusion, and that the world really consists of nothing but mind. In a rash moment, however, I turned from the disciples to the Master and found in Hegel himself a farrago of confusions and what seemed to me little better than puns. I therefore abandoned his philosophy.

For a time I found satisfaction in a doctrine derived, with modification, from Plato. According to Plato's doctrine, which I accepted only in a watered-down form, there is an unchanging timeless world of ideas of which the world presented to our senses is an imperfect copy. Mathematics, according to this doctrine, deals with the world of ideas and has in consequence an exactness and perfection which is absent from the everyday world. This kind of mathematical mysticism, which Plato derived from Pythagoras, appealed to me. But in the end I found myself obliged to abandon this doctrine also, and I have never since found religious satisfaction in any philosophical doctrine that I could accept.

Some Philosophical Contacts

WHEN I was very young I indulged, like other young people, in daydreams, but I was more fortunate than most in that some of them came true. One of my daydreams was of receiving flattering letters from learned foreigners who knew me only through my work. The first such letter that I actually received was something of a landmark. It was from the French philosopher Louis Couturat. He had written a big book on the mathematical infinite which I had reviewed with moderate praise. He wrote to tell me that when my book on the foundations of geometry was published he was given it to review and set to work "armed with a dictionary," for he knew hardly any English. The rest of his letter consisted of the sort of praise that I had dreamed of. I made friends with him and visited him first at Caen and then in Paris. Independently of each other, we both published books on Leibniz, I in 1900 and he in 1901. My book had suggested a quite new interpretation of Leibniz' philosophy which I based upon a rather small number of texts. I regarded these texts as important because they made Leibniz' system much more profound and coherent than those upon which the traditional views of that system were based. Couturat, without knowing of my work, went to

Hanover, where the Leibniz manuscripts were kept, and found innumerable unpublished papers which established the correctness of an interpretation closely similar to mine and no longer a matter of conjecture. But after this our paths diverged. He devoted himself to advocating an international language. Unfortunately, international languages are even more numerous than national ones. He did not like Esperanto, which was the general favorite, but preferred Ido. I learned from him that Esperantists (so at least he assured me) were wicked beyond all previous depths of human depravity, but I never examined his evidence. He said that Esperanto had the advantage of allowing the word *Esperantist* for which Ido provided no analogue. "But yes," I said, "there is the word *Idiot*." He, however, refused to have the advocates of Ido called idiots. He was killed by a lorry during the mobilization of 1914.

My first serious contact with the German learned world consisted in the reading of Kant, whom, while a student, I viewed with awed respect. My teachers told me to feel at least equal respect for Hegel, and I accepted their judgment until I read him. But when I read him I found his remarks in the philosophy of mathematics (which was the part of philosophy that most interested me) both ignorant and stupid. This led me to reject his philosophy, and at the same time, for somewhat different reasons, I rejected the philosophy of Kant. But while I was abandoning the traditional German philosophy I was becoming aware of the work of German mathematicians on the principles of mathematics, which was at that time very much better than any work on the subject elsewhere. I read avidly the work of Weierstrass and Dedekind which swept away great quantities of metaphysical lumber that had obstructed the foundations of mathematics ever since the time of Leibniz. More important than either of these, both intrinsically and in his influence on my work, was Georg Cantor. He developed the theory of infinite numbers in epoch-making work which showed amazing genius. The work was very difficult and for a long time I did not fully understand it. I copied it, almost word for word, into a note-book because I found that this slow mode of progression made it more intelligible. While I was doing so I thought his work fallacious, but nevertheless persisted. When I had fin-ished, I discovered that the fallacies had been mine and not his. He was a very eccentric man and, when he was not do-ing epoch-making work in mathematics, he was writing books to prove that Bacon wrote Shakespeare. He sent me one of these books with an inscription on the cover saying, "I see your motto is Kant or Cantor." Kant was his bugbear. In a letter to me he described him as, "Yonder sophistical Philistine who knew so little mathematics." He was a very pugnacious man and, when he was in the middle of a great controversy with the French mathematician Henri Poincaré, he wrote to me, "I shall not be the succumbent!" which in-deed proved to be the case. To my lasting regret, I never met him. Just at a moment when I was to have met him, his son fell ill and he had to return to Germany.

The influence of these men on my work belonged to the last years of the nineteenth century. With the beginning of the twentieth, I became aware of a man for whom I had and have the very highest respect although at that time he was practically unknown. This man is Frege. It is difficult to ac-count for the fact that his work did not receive recognition. Dedekind had been justly acclaimed, but Frege on the very same topics was much more profound. My relations with him were curious. They ought to have begun when my teacher in philosophy, James Ward, gave me Frege's little book *Begriffsschrift* saying that he had not read the book and did not know whether it had any value. To my shame I have to confess that I did not read it either, until I had independently worked out a great deal of what it contained. The book was published in 1879 and I read it in 1901. I rather suspect that I was its first reader. What first attracted me to Frege was a review of a later book of his by Peano accusing him of unnecessary subtlety. As Peano was the most subtle logician I had at that time come across, I felt that Frege must be remarkable. I acquired the first volume of his book on arithmetic (the second volume was not yet published). I read the introduction with passionate admiration, but I was repelled by the crabbed symbolism which he had invented and it was only after I had done the same work for myself that I was able to understand what he had written in the main text. He was the first to expound the view which was and is mine, that mathematics is a prolongation of logic, and he was the first to give a definition of numbers in logical terms. He did this in 1884 but nobody noticed that he had done it.

Frege thought, as I thought for a few months at the turn of the century, that the reduction of mathematics to logic had been definitively completed. But in June 1901 I came across a contradiction which proved that something was amiss. I wrote to Frege about it and he behaved with a noble candor which cannot be too highly praised. The second volume of his arithmetic had been passed through the press but not yet published. He added an appendix saying that in view of the contradiction that I had brought to his notice "*die Arithmetik ist ins Schwanken geraten.*" I understand that in later years, like the Pythagoreans when confronted with irrationals, he took refuge in geometrical treatment of arithmetic. In this I cannot follow him, but it is interesting to observe the repetition of ancient history in a new context. To my lasting regret, I never met Frege, but I am glad to have done all that lay in my power to win him the the recognition which he deserved.

An even more important philosophical contact was with the Austrian philosopher Ludwig Wittgenstein, who began as my pupil and ended as my supplanter at both Oxford and Cambridge. He had intended to become an engineer and had gone to Manchester for that purpose. The training for an engineer required mathematics, and he was thus led to interest in the foundations of mathematics. He inquired at Manchester whether there was such a subject and whether anybody worked at it. They told him about me, and so he came to Cambridge. He was queer, and his notions seemed to me odd, so that for a whole term I could not make up my mind whether he was a man of genius or merely an eccentric. At the end of his first term at Cambridge he came to me and said: "Will you please tell me whether I am a complete idiot or not?" I replied, "My dear fellow, I don't know. Why are you asking me?" He said, "Because, if I am a complete idiot, I shall become an aeronaut; but, if not, I shall become a philosopher." I told him to write me something during the vacation on some philosophical subject and I would then tell him whether he was complete idiot or not. At the beginning of the following term he brought me the fulfillment of this suggestion. After reading only one sentence, I said to him: "No, you must not become an aeronaut." And he didn't. He was not, however, altogether easy to deal with. He used to come to my rooms at midnight, and for hours he would walk backward and forward like a caged tiger. On arrival, he would announce that when he left my rooms he would commit suicide. So, in spite of getting sleepy, I did not like to turn him out. On one such evening, after an hour or two of dead silence, I said to him, "Wittgenstein, are you thinking about logic or about your sins?" "Both," he said, and then reverted to silence. However, we did not meet only at night. I used to take him long walks in the country round Cambridge. On one occasion I induced him to trespass with me in Madingley Wood where, to my surprise, he climbed a tree. When he had got a long way up a gamekeeper with a gun turned up and protested to me about the trespass. I called up to Wittgenstein and said the man had promised not to shoot if Wittgenstein got down within a minute. He believed me, and did so. In the First War he fought in the Austrian army and was taken prisoner by the Italians two days *after* the armistice. I had a letter from him from Monte Cassino, where he was interned, saying that fortunately he had had his manuscript with him when he was taken prisoner. This manuscript, which was published and became famous, had been written while he was at the front. He inherited a great fortune from his father, but he gave it away on the ground that money is only a nuisance to a philosopher. In order to earn his living, he became a village schoolmaster at a little place called Trattenbach, from which he wrote me an unhappy letter saying, "The men of Trattenbach are wicked." I replied, "All men are wicked." He rejoined, "True, but the men of Trattenbach are more wicked than the men of any other place." I retorted that my logical sense rebelled against such a statement; and there the matter rested until residence elsewhere enlarged his view as to the prevalence of sin. In his later years he was professor of philosophy at Cambridge, and most philosophers both there and at Oxford became his disciples. I myself was very much influenced by his earlier doctrines, but in later years our views increasingly diverged. I saw very little of him in his later years, but at the time when I knew him well he was immensely impressive as he had fire and penetration and intellectual purity to a quite extraordinary degree.

A man who impressed me, not so much by his ability as

by his resolute absorption in philosophy even under the most arduous circumstances, was the only Yugoslav philosopher of our time, whose name was Branislav Petronievic. I met him only once, in the year 1917. The only language we both knew was German and so we had to use it, although it caused people in the street to look at us with suspicion. The Serbs had recently carried out their heroic mass retreat before the German invaders, and I was anxious to get a firsthand account of this retreat from him, but he only wanted to expound his doctrine that the number of points in space is finite and can be estimated by considerations derived from the theory of numbers. The consequence of this difference in our interests was a somewhat curious conversation. I said, "Were you in the great retreat?" and he replied, "Yes, but you see the way to calculate the number of points in space is . . ." I said, "Were you on foot?" and he said, "Yes, you see the number must be a prime." I said, "Did you not try to get a horse?" and he said, "I started on a horse, but I fell off, and it should not be difficult to find out what prime." In spite of all my efforts, I could get nothing further from him about anything so trivial as the Great War. I admired his capacity for intellectual detachment from the accidents of his corporeal existence, in which I felt that few ancient Stoics could have rivaled him. After the First War he was employed by the Yugoslav Government to bring out a magnificent edition of the eighteenth-century Yugoslav philosopher Boscovic, but what happened to him after that I do not know.

These are only a few of the men who have influenced me. I can think of two who have influenced me even more. They are the Italian Peano, and my friend G. E. Moore.

Experiences of a Pacifist in the
First World War

M Y LIFE has been sharply divided into two periods, one before and one after the outbreak of the First World War, which shook me out of many prejudices and made me think afresh on a number of fundamental questions.

In common with other people I had observed with dismay the increasing danger of war. I disliked the policy of the Entente, which I first heard advocated in 1902 by Sir Edward Grey at a small discussion club of which I was a member. The policy had not then been adopted and Sir Edward Grey was not then in the Government, but he knew the Government's intentions and agreed with them. I protested vehemently. I did not like being aligned with Czarist Russia, and I saw no insurmountable obstacle to a *modus vivendi* with the Kaiser's Germany. I foresaw that a great war would mark the end of an epoch and drastically lower the general level of civilization. On these grounds I should have wished England to remain neutral. Subsequent history has confirmed me in this opinion.

During the hot days at the end of July, I was at Cambridge,

discussing the situation with all and sundry. I found it impossible to believe that Europe would be so mad as to plunge into war, but I was pursuaded that, if there was war, England would be involved. I collected signatures of a large number of professors and Fellows to a statement in favor of neutrality which appeared in the *Manchester Guardian*. The day war was declared, almost all of them changed their minds. Looking back, it seems extraordinary that one did not realize more clearly what was coming.

I spent the evening of August 4 walking round the streets, especially in the neighborhood of Trafalgar Square, noticing cheering crowds, and making myself sensitive to the emotions of passers-by. During this and the following days I discovered to my amazement that average men and women were delighted at the prospect of war. I had fondly imagined, what most Pacifists contended, that wars were forced upon a reluctant population by despotic and Machiavellian governments.

I was tortured by patriotism. The successes of the Germans before the Battle of the Marne were horrible to me. I desired the defeat of Germany as ardently as any retired colonel. Love of England is very nearly the strongest emotion I possess, and in appearing to set it aside at such a moment, I was making a very difficult renunciation. Nevertheless, I never had a moment's doubt as to what I must do. I have at times been paralyzed by skepticism, at times I have been cynical, at other times indifferent, but when the war came I felt as if I heard the voice of God. I knew that it was my business to protest, however futile protest might be. My whole nature was involved. As a lover of truth, the national propaganda of all the belligerent nations sickened me. As a lover of civilization, the return to barbarism appalled me. As a man of thwarted parental feeling, the massacre of the young wrung my heart. I hardly supposed that much good would come of opposing the war, but I felt that for the honor of human nature those who were not swept off their feet should show that they stood firm. After seeing troop trains departing from Waterloo, I used to have strange visions of London as a place of unreality. I used in imagination to see the bridges collapse and sink, and the whole great city vanish like a morning mist. Its inhabitants began to seem like hallucinations, and I would wonder whether the world in which I thought I had lived was a mere product of my own febrile nightmares. Such moods, however, were brief, and were put an end to by the need of work.

I addressed many Pacifist meetings, usually without incident, but there was one, in support of the Kerensky revolution, which was more violent. It was at the Brotherhood Church in Southgate Road. Patriotic newspapers distributed leaflets in all the neighboring public houses (the district is a very poor one) saying that we were in communication with the Germans and signaled to their airplanes as to where to drop bombs. This made us somewhat unpopular in the neighborhood, and a mob presently besieged the church. Most of us believed that resistance would be either wicked or unwise, since some of us were complete nonresisters, and others realized that we were too few to resist the whole surrounding slum population. A few people, among them Francis Meynell, attempted resistance, and I remember his returning from the door with his face streaming with blood. The mob burst in led by a few officers; all except the officers were more or less drunk. The fiercest were viragos who used wooden boards full of rusty nails. An attempt was made by the officers to induce the women among us to retire first so that they might deal as they thought fit with the Pacifist men, whom they supposed to be all cowards. Mrs. Snowden behaved on this occasion in a very admirable manner. She refused point-blank to leave the hall unless the men were allowed to leave at the same time. The other women present agreed with her. This rather upset the officers in charge of the roughs, as they did not particularly wish to assault women. But by this time the mob had its blood up, and pandemonium broke loose. Everybody had to escape as best they could while the police looked on calmly. Two of the drunken viragos began to attack me with their boards full of nails. While I was wondering how one defended oneself against this type of attack, one of the ladies among us went up to the police and suggested that they should defend me. The police, however, merely shrugged their shoulders. "But he is an eminent philosopher," said the lady, and the police still shrugged. "But he is famous all over the world as a man of learning," she continued. The police remained unmoved. "But he is the brother of an earl," she finally cried. At this, the police rushed to my assistance. They were, however, too late to be of any service, and I owe my life to a young woman whom I did not know, who interposed herself between me and the viragos long enough for me to make my escape. She, I am happy to say, owing to the police, was not attacked. But quite a number of people, including several women, had their clothes torn off their backs as they left the building.

The clergyman to whom the Brotherhood Church belonged was a pacifist of remarkable courage. In spite of this experience, he invited me on a subsequent occasion to give an address in his church. On this occasion, however, the mob set fire to the pulpit and the address was not delivered. These were the only occasions on which I came across personal violence; all my other meetings were undisturbed. But such is the power of Press propaganda that my non-pacifist friends came to me and said: "Why do you go on trying to address meetings when all of them are broken up by the mob?"

For four and a half months in 1918 I was in prison for Pacifist propaganda; but, by the intervention of Arthur Balfour, I was placed in the first division, so that while in prison I was able to read and write as much as I liked, provided I did no pacifist propaganda. I found prison in many ways quite agreeable. I had no engagements, no difficult decisions to make, no fear of callers, no interruptions to my work. I read enormously; I wrote a book, *Introduction to Mathematical Philosophy*, and began the work for *Analysis of Mind*. I was rather interested in my fellow prisoners, who seemed to me in no way morally inferior to the rest of the population, though they were on the whole slightly below the usual level of intelligence, as was shown by their having been caught. For anybody not in the first division, especially for a person accustomed to reading and writing, prison is a severe and terrible punishment; but for me, thanks to Arthur Balfour, this was not so. I was much cheered on my arrival by the warder at the gate, who had to take particulars about me. He asked my religion, and I replied "agnostic." He asked how to spell it, and remarked with a sigh: "Well, there are many religions, but I suppose they all worship the same God." This remark kept me cheerful for about a week.

I came out of prison in September 1918, when it was already clear that the war was ending. During the last weeks, in common with most other people, I based my hopes upon Wilson with his Fourteen Points and his League of Nations. The end of the war was so swift and dramatic that no one had time to adjust feelings to changed circumstances. I learned on the morning of November 11, a few hours in advance of the general public, that the armistice was coming. I went out into the street, and told a Belgian soldier, who said: *"Tiens, c'est chic!"* I went into a tobacconist's and told the lady who served me. "I am glad of that," she said, "because now we shall be able to get rid of the interned Germans." At eleven o'clock, when the armistice was announced, I was in Tottenham Court Road. Within two minutes, everybody in all the shops and offices had come into the street. They commandeered the buses, and made them go where they liked. I saw a man and woman, complete strangers to each other, meet in the middle of the road and kiss as they passed. The crowd rejoiced and I also rejoiced. But I remained as solitary as before.

From Logic to Politics

THE First World War shook me out of my prejudices and made me think afresh on a number of fundamental questions. It also provided me with a new kind of activity, for which I did not feel the staleness that beset me whenever I tried to return to mathematical logic. I have therefore got into the habit of thinking of myself as a non-supernatural Faust for whom Mephistopheles was represented by the First World War.

Although I did not completely abandon logic and abstract philosophy, I became more and more absorbed in social questions and especially in the causes of war and the possible ways of preventing it. I have found my work on such subjects much more difficult and much less successful than my earlier work on mathematical logic. It is difficult because its utility depends upon persuasion, and my previous training and experience had not been any help toward persuasiveness.

I had always been interested in social questions and had felt especially a horror of cruelty which made me very averse from war. There had been a time in the nineties when, under the influence of the Sidney Webbs, I had been more or less of an Imperialist and, at first, a supporter of the Boer War. But early in 1901 I had an experience not unlike what reli-

gious people call "conversion." I became suddenly and vividly aware of the loneliness in which most people live, and
passionately desirous of finding ways of diminishing this
tragic isolation. In the course of a few minutes I changed my
mind about the Boer War, about harshness in education and
in the criminal law, and about combativeness in private relations. I expressed the outcome of this experience in *A Free
Man's Worship*. But I was absorbed, with my friend Whitehead, in the herculean task of writing *Principia Mathematica*,
a book which occupied the best energies of us both for a period of ten years. The completion of this task left me with
a new degree of mental freedom, and therefore ready intellectually as well as emotionally for the redirection of my
thoughts that was brought about by the war.

During the first days of the war, I was struck by the importance of the connection of politics and individual psychology. What masses of men agree to do is the result of passions
which they feel in common, and these passions, as I was suddenly compelled to realize, are not those that I found
emphasized by most political theorists. I was at that time completely ignorant of psychoanalysis, but observation of war-
like crowds inspired me with thoughts having much affinity
with those of psychoanalysts, as I afterward discovered. I
saw that a peaceful world cannot be built on a basis of populations that enjoy fighting and killing. I thought I saw also
what kinds of inward and outward defeat lead people to impulses of violence and cruelty. It seemed to me that no reform could be stable unless it altered the feelings of individuals. The feelings of adult individuals are a product of many
causes: experiences in infancy; education; economic struggles; and success or frustration in private relations. Men, on
the average, will be kindly or hostile in their feelings toward
each other in proportion as they feel their lives successful or

unsuccessful. This of course does not apply to everybody. There are saints who can endure misfortune without becoming embittered, and there are fierce men whom no success will soften. But politics depends mainly upon the average mass of mankind; and the average mass will be fierce or kindly according to circumstances. Ever since those first days in August 1914, I have been firmly convinced that the only stable improvements in human affairs are those which increase kindly feeling and diminish ferocity.

When I visited Russia in 1920, I found there a philosophy very different from my own, a philosophy based upon hatred and force and despotic power. I had become isolated from conventional opinion by my views on the war, and I became isolated from left-wing opinion by my profound horror of what was being done in Russia. I remained in a political solitude until, bit by bit, left-wing opinion in the West became aware that the Russian Communists were not creating a paradise.

In the Marxist philosophy, as interpreted in Moscow, I found, as I believe, two enormous errors, one of theory and one of feeling. The error of theory consisted in believing that the only undesirable form of power over other human beings is economic power, and that economic power is co-extensive with ownership. In this theory other forms of power—military, political and propagandist—are ignored, and it is forgotten that the power of a large economic organization is concentrated in a small executive, and not diffused among all the nominal owners or shareholders. It was therefore supposed that exploitation and oppression must disappear if the State became the sole capitalist, and it was not realized that this would confer upon State officials all, and more than all, the powers of oppression formerly possessed by individual capitalists. The other error, which was concerned with feeling, consisted in supposing that a good state of affairs can be brought about by a movement of which the motive force is hate. Those who had been inspired mainly by hatred of capitalists and landowners had acquired the habit of hating, and after achieving victory were impelled to look for new objects of detestation. Hence came, by a natural psychological mechanism, the purges, the massacre of Kulaks, and the forced labor camps. I am persuaded that Lenin and his early colleagues were actuated by a wish to benefit mankind, but from errors in psychology and political theory they created a hell instead of a heaven. This was to me a profoundly important object lesson in the necessity of right thinking and right feeling if any good result is to be achieved in the organization of human relations.

After my brief visit to Russia, I spent nearly a year in China, where I became more vividly aware than before of the vast problems concerned with Asia. China at that time was in a condition of anarchy; and, while Russia had too much government, China had too little. There was much that I found admirable in the Chinese tradition, but it was obvious that none of this could survive the onslaughts promoted by Western and Japanese rapacity. I fully expected to see China transformed into a modern industrial State as fierce and militaristic as the Powers that it was compelled to resist. I expected that in due course there would be in the world only three first-class Powers—America, Russia and China—and that the new China would possess none of the merits of the old. These expectations are now being fulfilled.

I have never been able to believe wholeheartedly in any simple nostrum by which all ills are to be cured. On the contrary, I have come to think that one of the main causes of trouble in the world is dogmatic and fanatical belief in some doctrine for which there is no adequate evidence. Nationalism, Fascism, Communism, and now anti-Communism have all produced their crop of bigoted zealots ready to work untold horror in the interests of some narrow creed. All such fanaticisms have in a greater or less degree the defect which I found in the Moscow Marxists, namely, that their dynamic power is largely due to hate.

Throughout my life I have longed to feel that oneness with large bodies of human beings that is experienced by the members of enthusiastic crowds. The longing has often been strong enough to lead me into self-deception. I have imagined myself in turn a Liberal, a Socialist, or a Pacifist, but I have never been any of these things in any profound sense. Always the skeptical intellect, when I have most wished it silent, has whispered doubts to me, has cut me off from the facile enthusiasms of others, and has transported me into a desolate solitude. During the First War, while I worked with Quakers, nonresisters and Socialists, while I was willing to accept unpopularity and the inconvenience belonging to unpopular opinions, I would tell the Quakers that I thought many wars in history had been justified, and the Socialists that I dreaded the tyranny of the State. They would look askance at me, and while continuing to accept my help would feel that I was not one of them. Underlying all occupations and all pleasures, I felt from early youth the pain of solitude. This feeling of isolation, however, has grown much less since 1939, for during the last fifteen years I have been broadly in agreement with most of my compatriots on important issues.

The world since 1914 has developed in ways very different from what I should have desired. Nationalism has increased, militarism has increased, liberty has diminished. Large parts of the world are less civilized than they were. Victory in two great wars has much diminished the good things for which we fought. All thinking and feeling is overshadowed by the dread of a new war worse than either of its predecessors. No limit can be seen to the possibilities of scientific destruction. But, in spite of these causes for apprehension, there are reasons, though less obvious ones, for cautious hope. It would now be technically possible to unify the world and abolish war altogether. It would also be technically possible to abolish poverty completely. These things would be done if men desired their own happiness more than the misery of their enemies. There were, in the past, physical obstacles to human well-being. The only obstacles now are in the souls of men. Hatred, folly and mistaken beliefs alone stand between us and the millennium. While they persist, they threaten us with unprecedented disaster. But perhaps the very magnitude of the peril may frighten the world into common sense.

Beliefs: Discarded and Retained

I BEGAN to develop a philosophy of my own during the year 1898, when, with encouragement from my friend G. E. Moore, I threw over the doctrines of Hegel. If you watch a bus approaching you during a bad London fog, you see first a vague blur of extra darkness, and you only gradually become aware of it as a vehicle with parts and passengers. According to Hegel, your first view as a vague blur is more correct than your later impression, which is inspired by the misleading impulses of the analytic intellect. This point of view was temperamentally unpleasing to me. Like the philosophers of ancient Greece, I prefer sharp outlines and definite separations such as the landscapes of Greece afford. When I first threw over Hegel, I was delighted to be able to believe in the bizarre multiplicity of the world. I thought to myself, "Hegel says there is only the One, but there really *are* twelve categories in Kant's philosophy." It may seem queer that this was the example of plurality that specially impressed me, but I am concerned to report the facts without distortion.

For some years after throwing over Hegel I had an optimistic riot of opposite beliefs. I thought that whatever Hegel had denied must be true. He had maintained that there is no absolute truth. The nearest approach (so he maintained) to absolute truth is truth about the Absolute; but even that is not quite true, because it unduly separates subject and object. Consequently I, in rebellion, maintained that there are innumerable absolute truths, more particularly in mathematics. Hegel had maintained that all separateness is illusory and that the universe is more like a pot of treacle than a heap of shot. I therefore said, "the universe is exactly like a heap of shot." Each separate shot, according to the creed I then held, had hard and precise boundaries and was as absolute as Hegel's Absolute. Hegel had professed to prove by logic that number, space, time and matter are illusions, but I developed a new logic which enabled me to think that these things were as real as any mathematician could wish. I read a paper to a philosophical congress in Paris in 1900 in which I argued that there really are points and instants. Broadly speaking, I took the view that, whenever Hegel's proof that some thing does not exist is invalid, one may assume that the something in question does exist—at any rate when that assumption is convenient to the mathematician. Pythagoras and Plato had let their views of the universe be shaped by mathematics, and I followed them gaily.

It was Whitehead who was the serpent in this paradise of Mediterranean clarity. He said to me once: "You think the world is what it looks like in fine weather at noon day; I think it is what it seems like in the early morning when one first wakes from deep sleep." I thought his remark horrid, but could not see how to prove that my bias was any better than his. At last he showed me how to apply the technique of mathematical logic to his vague and higgledy-piggledy world, and dress it up in Sunday clothes that the mathematician could view without being shocked. This technique which I learned from him delighted me, and I no longer demanded that the naked truth should be as good as the truth in its mathematical Sunday best.

Although I still think that this is scientifically the right way to deal with the world, I have come to think that the mathematical and logical wrappings in which the naked truth is dressed go to deeper layers than I had supposed, and that things which I had thought to be skin are only well-made garments. Take, for instance, numbers: when you count, you count "things," but "things" have been invented by human beings for their own convenience. This is not obvious on the earth's surface because, owing to the low temperature, there is a certain degree of apparent stability. But it would be obvious if one could live on the sun where there is nothing but perpetually changing whirlwinds of gas. If you lived on the sun, you would never have formed the idea of "things," and you would never have thought of counting because there would be nothing to count. In such an environment, Hegel's philosophy would seem to be common sense, and what we consider common sense would appear as fantastic metaphysical speculation.

Such reflections have led me to think of mathematical exactness as a human dream, and not as an attribute of an approximately knowable reality. I used to think that of course there is exact truth about anything, though it may be difficult and perhaps impossible to ascertain it. Suppose, for example, that you have a rod which you know to be about a yard long. In the happy days when I retained my mathematical faith, I should have said that your rod certainly *is* longer than a yard or shorter than a yard or exactly a yard long. Now I should admit that some rods can be known to be longer than a yard and some can be known to be shorter than a yard, but none can be known to be exactly a yard, and, indeed, the phrase "exactly a yard" has no definite meaning.

Exactness, in fact, was a Hellenic myth which Plato located in heaven. He was right in thinking that it can find no home on earth. To my mathematical soul, which is attuned by nature to the visions of Pythagoras and Plato, this is a sorrow. I try to console myself with the knowledge that mathematics is still the necessary implement for the manipulation of nature. If you want to make a battleship or a bomb, if you want to develop a kind of wheat which will ripen farther north than any previous variety, it is to mathematics that you must turn. You can kill a man with a battle-ax or with a surgeon's knife; either is equally effective. Mathematics, which had seemed like a surgeon's knife, is really more like the battle-ax. But it is only in applications to the real world that mathematics has the crudity of the battle-ax. Within its own sphere, it retains the neat exactness of the surgeon's knife. The world of mathematics and logic remains, in its own domain delightful; but it is the domain of imagination. Mathematics must live, with music and poetry, in the region of man-made beauty, not amid the dust and grime of the world.

I said a moment ago that, in revolt against Hegel, I came to think of the world as more like a heap of shot than a pot of treacle. I still think that, on the whole, this view is right; but I gradually discovered that some things which I had taken to be solid shots in the heap did not deserve this dignity. In the first flush of my belief in separate atoms, I thought that every word that can be used significantly must signify something, and I took this to mean that it must signify some *thing*. But the words that most interest logicians are difficult from this point of view. They are such words as "if" and "or" and "not." I tried to believe that in some logicians' limbo there are things that these words mean, and that perhaps virtuous logicians may meet them hereafter in a more logical cosmos. I felt fairly satisfied about "or" and "if" and "not," but I hesitated about such words as "nevertheless." My queer zoo contained some very odd monsters, such as the golden mountain and the present King of France—monsters which, although they roamed my zoo at will, had the odd property of nonexistence. There are still a number of philosophers who believe this sort of thing, and it is their beliefs which have become the philosophical basis of Existentialism. But, for my part, I came to think that many words and phrases have no significance in isolation, but only contribute to the significance of whole sentences. I have therefore ceased to hope to meet "if" and "or" and "not" in heaven. I was able, in fact, by the roundabout road of a complicated technique, to return to views much nearer to those of common sense than my previous speculations.

In spite of such changes, I have retained a very large part of the logical beliefs that I had fifty-five years ago. I am persuaded that the world is made up of an immense number of bits, and that, so far as logic can show, each bit might be exactly as it is even if other bits did not exist. I reject wholly the Hegelian argument that all reality must be mental. I do not think one *can* argue as to what reality must be. When Whitehead persuaded me that the mathematician's space and time are polished man-made tools, he did not persuade me, and I believe did not himself think, that there is nothing in nature out of which these tools are made. I still think that what we can know about the world outside the thoughts and feelings of living beings, we can know only through physical science. I still think that what we can know of the world, we can know only by observation and not by complicated arguments as to what it must be.

Throughout the time during which mathematical logic was my chief preoccupation, I was nevertheless keenly interested in social questions, and occupied myself with them in my spare time. I campaigned against tariff reform and in favor of votes for women. I stood for Parliament, and worked at General Elections. But it was not until 1914 that social questions became my main preoccupation.

Hopes: Realized and Disappointed

URING the eighty-two years of my life the world has changed as much as in any equal period of human history, if not more. It had, when I was young, an apparently stable pattern, which was not expected to alter fundamentally but only to undergo the sort of gradual evolution which had taken place in England. There were the Great Powers, which were European. (Most people forgot the United States, still recovering from the Civil War.) All the Great Powers except France were monarchies, and France only ceased to be a monarchy two years before I was born. When I first became politically conscious, Disraeli was Prime Minister and the country was indulging in a honeymoon of Imperialism. It was at this time that Queen Victoria became Empress of India, and that the Prime Minister boasted of having secured peace with honor. The "peace" consisted of not going to war with Russia; the "honor" consisted of the island of Cyprus which is now causing us first-rate embarrassment. It was in these years that the word Jingo was coined. The far-flung might of Britain was displayed in the Afghan War, the Zulu War, and the First Boer War. All these I was taught to disapprove of, and I was indoctrinated with the creed of the Little Englander. But this creed was

44

never wholly sincere. Even the littlest of Little Englanders rejoiced in England's prowess. The power and prestige of the aristocracy and the landed gentry were unimpaired. When my uncle married the daughter of a great industrial magnate, my grandmother was proud of her liberality in not objecting to his marrying into what she called "Trade." Outside of Britain, the scene was dominated by the three great Eastern Empires of Germany, Austria and Russia. Nobody thought of them as transitory, although the German Empire had come into existence only a year before I was born and the Russian Empire (so Western liberals thought) would have to adopt a parliamentary constitution sooner or later.

I grew up as an ardent believer in optimistic liberalism. I both hoped and expected to see throughout the world a gradual spread of parliamentary democracy, personal liberty, and freedom for the countries that were at that time subject to European Powers, including Britain. I hoped that everybody would in time see the wisdom of Cobden's arguments for Free Trade, and that nationalism might gradually fade into a universal humanism. My parents, as disciples of John Stuart Mill, objected to the subjection of women, and I wholeheartedly followed them in this respect. Although, in the years before 1914, threatening clouds appeared upon the horizon, it still was possible to remain optimistic and to hope that diplomatic adjustments would prevent a catastrophe.

The things which I thought good in those days, I still think good. But, although some of them have come to pass, others seem very much more distant than they did in that happy age. On the whole, internal developments in Britain have been such as I could welcome. Democracy had been completed by the giving of votes to women. Moderate Socialism has been adopted within such limits as are not fatal to individual liberty. In the sphere of private morality, there is much more tolerance than there was in Victorian days. The standard of life among wage-earners has been greatly raised. The death rate, and especially the infant death rate, has been enormously reduced without producing a catastrophic increase of population. All these are vast improvements, and I have very little doubt that in time of peace the average level of happiness in Britain is a great deal higher than it was when I was young.

But when we pass to the international scene, the picture is very different. The old despotism of the Czars, at which liberals used to shudder, has been succeeded by a far more intense and cruel despotism. The old Austrian Empire, which oppressed subject nationalities and had been the very symbol of reaction, has been replaced over most of its territory by a new and more rigorous oppression imposed from Moscow. China, after a long period of go-as-you-please anarchy, is being welded in a great crucible of suffering into an infinitely formidable weapon of military power. The United States, which was to my parents the Mecca of Liberalism, is now in danger of becoming quite the opposite—though there is still hope that the danger may be averted. And over all hangs the appalling terror of atomic war.

This is such a different world from that of Victorian optimism that it is not altogether easy for a man who grew up in the one age to adjust himself to the other. It is a temptation to abandon hopes of which the realization seems distant and difficult. In the lassitude of temporary defeat, it may seem no longer worth while to keep intact a belief in values that once seemed inestimable. Perhaps a well-ordered prison is all that the human race deserves—so at least the Devil whispers in moments of discouragement. But some fundamental pride rebels against such insidious suggestions. I will not submit my judgments as to what is good and what is bad to the chance arbitrament of the momentary course of events. I will not praise armies of slaves because they can win battles. The dangers are new and the measures required to avert them are unprecedented, but that is no reason for a change in one's estimate as to what makes a good life or a good community.

A readiness to adapt oneself to the facts of the real world is often praised as a virtue, and in part it is. It is a bad thing to close one's eyes to facts or to fail to admit them because they are unwelcome. But it is also a bad thing to assume that whatever is in the ascendant must be right, that regard for fact demands subservience to evil. Even worse than conscious subservience to evil is the self-deception which denies that it is evil. When I find individual liberty being everywhere lessened by regimentation, I will not on that account pretend that regimentation is a good thing. It may be necessary for a time, but one should not on that account acquiesce in it as part of any society that one can admire.

I still want, and I still hope to see realized sooner or later, both for the individual and for the community, the same sort of things that I thought good when I was young. I think I should put first, security against extreme disaster such as that threatened by modern war. I should put second, the abolition of abject poverty throughout the world. Third, as a result of security and economic well-being, a general growth of tolerance and kindly feeling. Fourth, the greatest possible opportunity for personal initiative in ways not harmful to the community. All these things are possible, and all would come about if men chose. In the meantime, the human race lives in a welter of organized hatreds and threats of mutual extermination. I cannot but think that sooner or later people will grow tired of this very uncomfortable way of living. A person who lived so in private life would be considered a lunatic. If I bought a revolver and threatened to shoot my next-door neighbor, he would also no doubt buy a revolver to protect himself if he lived in a community where law and police did not exist. He and I would both find life much more unpleasant than it is at present, but we should not be acting any more absurdly than the present States which are guided by the supposedly best wisdom that human beings can provide.

When I come to what I myself can do or ought to do about the world situation, I find myself in two minds. A perpetual argument goes on within me between two different points of view which I will call that of the Devil's Advocate and that of the Earnest Publicist. My family during four centuries was important in the public life of England, and I was brought up to feel a responsibility which demanded that I should express my opinion on political questions. This feeling is more deeply implanted in me than reason would warrant, and the voice of the Devil's Advocate is, at least in part, the voice of reason. "Can't you see," says this cynical character, "that what happens in the world does not depend upon you? Whether the populations of the world are to live or die rests with the decisions of Khrushchev, Mao Tse-tung and Mr. John Foster Dulles, not with ordinary mortals like ourselves. If they say 'die,' we shall die. If they say 'live,' we shall live. They do not read your books, and would think them very silly if they did. You forget that you are not living in 1688, when your family and a few others gave the king notice and hired another. It is only a failure to move with the times that makes you bother your head with public affairs." Perhaps the Devil's Advocate is right—but perhaps he is wrong. Perhaps dictators are not so all-powerful as they seem; perhaps public opinion can still sway them, at any rate in some degree; and perhaps books can help to create public opinion. And so I persist, regardless of his taunts. There are limits to his severities. "Well, at any rate," he says, "writing books is an innocent occupation and it keeps you out of mischief." And so I go on writing books, though whether any good will come of doing so, I do not know.

How to Grow Old

IN SPITE of the title, this article will really be on how *not* to grow old, which, at my time of life, is a much more important subject. My first advice would be to choose your ancestors carefully. Although both my parents died young, I have done well in this respect as regards my other ancestors. My maternal grandfather, it is true, was cut off in the flower of his youth at the age of sixty-seven, but my other three grandparents all lived to be over eighty. Of remoter ancestors I can only discover one who did not live to a great age, and he died of a disease which is now rare, namely, having his head cut off. A great-grandmother of mine, who was a friend of Gibbon, lived to the age of ninety-two, and to her last day remained a terror to all her descendants. My maternal grandmother, after having nine children who survived, one who died in infancy, and many miscarriages, as soon as she became a widow devoted herself to women's higher education. She was one of the founders of Girton College, and worked hard at opening the medical profession to women. She used to relate how she met in Italy an elderly gentleman who was looking very sad. She inquired the cause of his melancholy and he said that he had just parted from his two grandchildren. "Good gracious," she exclaimed, "I have seventy-two grandchildren, and if I were sad each time I parted from one of them, I should have a dismal existence!" "Madre snaturale," he replied. But speaking as one of the seventy-two, I prefer her recipe. After the age of eighty she found she had some difficulty in getting to sleep, so she habitually spent the hours from midnight to 3:00 A.M. in reading popular science. I do not believe that she ever had time to notice that she was growing old. This, I think, is the proper recipe for remaining young. If you have wide and keen interests and activities in which you can still be effective, you will have no reason to think about the merely statistical fact of the number of years you have already lived, still less of the probable brevity of your future.

As regards health, I have nothing useful to say since I have little experience of illness. I eat and drink whatever I like, and sleep when I cannot keep awake. I never do anything whatever on the ground that it is good for health, though in actual fact the things I like doing are mostly wholesome.

Psychologically there are two dangers to be guarded against in old age. One of these is undue absorption in the past. It does not do to live in memories, in regrets for the good old days, or in sadness about friends who are dead. One's thoughts must be directed to the future, and to things about which there is something to be done. This is not always easy; one's own past is a gradually increasing weight. It is easy to think to oneself that one's emotions used to be more vivid than they are, and one's mind more keen. If this is true it should be forgotten, and if it is forgotten it will probably not be true.

The other thing to be avoided is clinging to youth in the hope of sucking vigor from its vitality. When your children are grown up they want to live their own lives, and if you continue to be as interested in them as you were when they were young, you are likely to become a burden to them, unless they are unusually callous. I do not mean that one should be without interest in them, but one's interest should be contemplative and, if possible, philanthropic, but not unduly emotional. Animals become indifferent to their young as soon as their young can look after themselves, but human beings, owing to the length of infancy, find this difficult.

I think that a successful old age is easiest for those who have strong impersonal interests involving appropriate activities. It is in this sphere that long experience is really fruitful, and it is in this sphere that the wisdom born of experience can be exercised without being oppressive. It is no use telling grown-up children not to make mistakes, both because they will not believe you, and because mistakes are an essential part of education. But if you are one of those who are incapable of impersonal interests, you may find that your life will be empty unless you concern yourself with your children and grandchildren. In that case you must realize that while you can still render them material services, such as making them an allowance or knitting them jumpers, you must not expect that they will enjoy your company.

Some old people are oppressed by the fear of death. In the young there is a justification for this feeling. Young men who have reason to fear that they will be killed in battle may justifiably feel bitter in the thought that they have been cheated of the best things that life has to offer. But in an old man who has known human joys and sorrows, and has achieved whatever work it was in him to do, the fear of death is somewhat abject and ignoble. The best way to overcome it—so at least it seems to me—is to make your interests gradually wider and more impersonal, until bit by bit the walls of the ego recede, and your life becomes increasingly merged in the universal life. An individual human existence should be like a river—small at first, narrowly contained within its banks, and rushing passionately past boulders and over waterfalls. Gradually the river grows wider, the banks recede, the waters flow more quietly, and in the end, without any visible break, they become merged in the sea, and painlessly lose their individual being. The man who, in old age, can see his life in this way, will not suffer from the fear of death, since the things he cares for will continue. And if, with the decay of vitality, weariness increases, the thought of rest will be not unwelcome. I should wish to die while still at work, knowing that others will carry on what I can no longer do, and content in the thought that what was possible has been done.

[Reprinted from *New Hopes for a Changing World*]

Reflections on
My Eightieth Birthday

O N REACHING the age of eighty it is reasonable to suppose that the bulk of one's work is done, and that what remains to do will be of less importance. The serious part of my life ever since boyhood has been devoted to two different objects which for a long time remained separate and have only in recent years united into a single whole. I wanted, on the one hand, to find out whether anything could be known; and, on the other hand, to do whatever might be possible toward creating a happier world. Up to the age of thirty-eight I gave most of my energies to the first of these tasks. I was troubled by skepticism and unwillingly forced to the conclusion that most of what passes for knowledge is open to reasonable doubt. I wanted certainty in the kind of way in which people want religious faith. I thought that certainty is more likely to be found in mathematics than elsewhere. But I discovered that many mathematical demonstrations, which my teachers expected me to accept, were full of fallacies, and that, if certainty were indeed discoverable in mathematics, it would be in a new kind of mathematics, with more solid foundations than those that had hitherto been thought secure. But as the work proceeded, I was continually reminded of the fable about the elephant and the tortoise. Having constructed an elephant upon which the mathematical world could rest, I found the elephant tottering, and proceeded to construct a tortoise to keep the elephant from falling. But the tortoise was no more secure than the elephant, and after some twenty years of very arduous toil, I came to the conclusion that there was nothing more that *I* could do in the way of making mathematical knowledge indubitable. Then came the First World War, and my thoughts became concentrated on human misery and folly. Neither misery nor folly seems to me any part of the inevitable lot of man. And I am convinced that intelligence, patience, and eloquence can, sooner or later, lead the human race out of its self-imposed tortures provided it does not exterminate itself meanwhile.

On the basis of this belief, I have had always a certain degree of optimism, although, as I have grown older, the optimism has grown more sober and the happy issue more distant. But I remain completely incapable of agreeing with those who accept fatalistically the view that man is born to trouble. The causes of unhappiness in the past and in the present are not difficult to ascertain. There have been poverty, pestilence, and famine, which were due to man's inadequate mastery of nature. There have been wars, oppressions and tortures which have been due to men's hostility to their fellow men. And there have been morbid miseries fostered by gloomy creeds, which have led men into profound inner discords that made all outward prosperity of no avail. All these are unnecessary. In regard to all of them, means are known by which they can be overcome. In the modern world, if communities are unhappy, it is because they choose to be so. Or, to speak more precisely, because they have ignorances, habits, beliefs, and passions, which are dearer to them than happiness or even life. I find many men in our dangerous age who seem to be in love with misery and death, and who grow angry when hopes are suggested to them. They think that hope is irrational and that, in sitting down to lazy despair, they are merely facing facts. I cannot agree with these men. To preserve hope in our world makes calls upon our intelligence and our energy. In those who despair it is very frequently the energy that is lacking.

The last half of my life has been lived in one of those painful epochs of human history during which the world is getting worse, and past victories which had seemed to be definitive have turned out to be only temporary. When I was young, Victorian optimism was taken for granted. It was thought that freedom and prosperity would spread gradually throughout the world by an orderly process, and it was hoped that cruelty, tyranny, and injustice would continually diminish. Hardly anyone was haunted by the fear of great wars. Hardly anyone thought of the nineteenth century as a brief interlude between past and future barbarism. For those who grew up in that atmosphere, adjustment to the world of the present has been difficult. It has been difficult not only emotionally but intellectually. Ideas that had been thought adequate have proved inadequate. In some directions valuable freedoms have proved very hard to preserve. In other directions, specially as regards relations between nations, freedoms formerly valued have proved potent sources of disaster. New thoughts, new hopes, new freedoms, and new restrictions upon freedom are needed if the world is to emerge from its present perilous state.

I cannot pretend that what I have done in regard to social and political problems has had any great importance. It is comparatively easy to have an immense effect by means of a dogmatic and precise gospel, such as that of Communism. But for my part I cannot believe that what mankind needs is anything either precise or dogmatic. Nor can I believe with any wholeheartedness in any partial doctrine which deals only with some part or aspect of human life. There are those who hold that everything depends upon institutions, and that good institutions will inevitably bring the millennium. And, on the other hand, there are those who believe that what is needed is a change of heart, and that, in comparison, institutions are of little account. I cannot accept either view. Institutions mold character, and character transforms institutions. Reforms in both must march hand in hand. And if individuals are to retain that measure of initiative and flexibility which they ought to have, they must not be all forced into one rigid mold; or, to change the metaphor, all drilled into one army. Diversity is essential in spite of the fact that it precludes universal acceptance of a single gospel. But to preach such a doctrine is difficult especially in arduous times. And perhaps it cannot be effective until some bitter lessons have been learned by tragic experience.

My work is near its end, and the time has come when I can survey it as a whole. How far have I succeeded, and how far have I failed? From an early age I thought of myself as dedicated to great and arduous tasks. Sixty-one years ago, walking alone in the Tiergarten through melting snow under the coldly glittering March sun, I determined to write two series of books: one abstract, growing gradually more concrete; the other concrete, growing gradually more abstract. They were to be crowned by a synthesis, combining pure theory with a practical social philosophy. Except for the final synthesis, which still eludes me, I have written these books. They have been acclaimed and praised, and the thoughts of many men and women have been affected by them. To this extent I have succeeded.

But as against this must be set two kinds of failure, one outward, one inward.

To begin with the outward failure: the Tiergarten has become a desert; the Brandenburger Tor, through which I entered it on that March morning, has become the boundary of two hostile empires, glaring at each other across an almost invisible barrier, and grimly preparing the ruin of mankind. Communists, Fascists, and Nazis have successively challenged all that I thought good, and in defeating them much of what their opponents have sought to preserve is being lost. Freedom has come to be thought weakness, and tolerance has been compelled to wear the garb of treachery. Old ideals are judged irrelevant, and no doctrine free from harshness commands respect.

The inner failure, though of little moment to the world, has made my mental life a perpetual battle. I set out with a more or less religious belief in a Platonic eternal world, in which mathematics shone with a beauty like that of the last Cantos of the Paradiso. I came to the conclusion that the eternal world is trivial, and that mathematics is only the art of saying the same thing in different words. I set out with a belief that love, free and courageous, could conquer the world without fighting. I ended by supporting a bitter and terrible war. In these respects there was failure.

But beneath all this load of failure I am still conscious of something that I feel to be victory. I may have conceived theoretical truth wrongly, but I was not wrong in thinking that there is such a thing, and that it deserves our allegiance. I may have thought the road to a world of free and happy human beings shorter than it is proving to be, but I was not wrong in thinking that such a world is possible, and that it is worth while to live with a view to bringing it nearer. I have lived in the pursuit of a vision, both personal and social. Personal: to care for what is noble, for what is beautiful, for what is gentle; to allow moments of insight to give wisdom at more mundane times. Social: to see in imagination the society that is to be created, where individuals grow freely, and where hate and greed and envy die because there is nothing to nourish them. These things I believe, and the world, for all its horrors, has left me unshaken.

Some Cambridge Dons of

the Nineties

IT IS now sixty-six years since I went up to Cambridge. The world in those days was a more leisurely place than it is now, and Cambridge was a much more leisurely place. From the point of view of an irreverent undergraduate the Dons of that time belonged to one or other of three not quite separate classes: there were figures of fun; there were men who were technically competent but uninteresting; and there was a small class of men whom we, the young, admired wholeheartedly and enthusiastically.

Some of the oddities, it must be said, were very odd. There was a Fellow who had a game leg and was known to be addicted to the amiable practice of putting the poker in the fire and when it became red-hot running after his guests with a view to murder. I discovered at last that he was only roused to homicidal fury when people sneezed. Owing to his game leg, those whom he attacked always escaped, and nobody minded his little peculiarities. I used to go to tea with him myself but I went away if I saw him put the poker into the fire. Except in his moments of aberration he was charming, and it never occurred to anyone to place him under restraint.

My mathematical coach was less fortunate. He went mad, but none of his pupils noticed it. At last he had to be shut up. That, however, was exceptional.

At a somewhat lower level of oddity, there were the two rivals for the honor of entertaining the Empress Frederick, namely Oscar Browning (always known as O. B.) and the Professor of Fine Arts. The latter was the more successful. He said to me on one occasion, "It really was most annoying that, in spite of all I could do to dissuade her, the Empress Frederick insisted on lunching with me a *second* time." On the evening of that same day, O. B. sighed wearily and said, "I've been Empress-hunting all day." He found it very difficult to admit that there were any Royalties whom he did not know personally. The nearest he ever came to it was in saying of the King of Saxony: "I knew him very well—by sight." There were endless stories about O. B. He was fat, tubby and unusually ugly. But malicious undergraduates, by purchasing large numbers of a certain picture paper, secured him the second prize in a beauty competition. (I myself heard him boast of this prize.) It was said that Tennyson, on a visit to Cambridge, had been entertained by the Fellows of Kings, who came up one by one, mentioning their names. When O. B. came up and said, "I'm Browning," Tennyson looked at him and said, "You're not." But I cannot vouch for the truth of this story.

The really fine flower of perfect Don-ishness was already passing away when I was an undergraduate, but I used to hear stories of it from older contemporaries. There was the Don who, whenever any reform was proposed, made exactly the same speech. He would say: "When a measure of this kind is suggested, I ask myself two questions: 'Has the old system worked badly?' 'Is the new system likely to work better?' I see no reason to answer either question in the affirmative, and I shall therefore vote against the proposal." Then there was the Don who disliked the subversive suggestion that Fellows henceforth need not be in Orders. Some rash men had maintained that the clerical and educational duties of Fellows might interfere with each other. He rebutted this argument with the words: "When the Roman Emperor assumed the Purple, it was the custom to make him a member of the College of Augurs. But it was not expected that he should feed the Sacred Chickens." This rich vintage was exhausted before my day. The nearest approach that I can remember was the Professor of Arabic who, to everybody's surprise, voted Liberal. When asked why, he replied: "Because when Mr. Gladstone is in office, he has no time to write about Holy Scripture."

The oddities, however, were exceptional. The great majority of Dons did their work competently without being either laughable or interesting. Sometimes, however, even among them rare merit would suddenly emerge. I remember a mathematical lecturer whom I had always thought quite uninteresting. He was lecturing on hydrostatics, working out a problem about a vessel with a lid rotating in a bathtub. One of the pupils said, "Haven't you forgotten the centrifugal forces on the lid?" The lecturer gasped and replied, "I've worked out this problem that way for twenty years. But you're right." From that moment we all felt a new respect for him.

The Dons, whom my contemporaries and I profoundly respected, had a great influence upon us, even sometimes when we had nothing to do with them in the way of work. There was, for example, Verrall, whose specialty was Euripides. He was brilliantly witty in a rather academic style. When Granville Barker was going to produce one of Gilbert Murray's translations of Euripides, he came to Cambridge to ask Verrall what a Mycenaean hut looked like. Verrall replied, "No one knows, but Miss Harrison will tell you." He became a victim of arthritis, which gradually deprived him of the use first of his legs and then of other muscles. In spite of intense pain, he continued to display exactly the same kind of rather glittering wit, and, so long as the power of speech remained with him, did not allow physical disability to affect his mind or his outlook. His wife was a believer in spiritualism and used to bring him masses of nonsensical script obtained by automatic writing. His practice in making sense out of Greek manuscripts enabled him to emend these scripts until they seemed to have sense. But I am afraid his attitude was not as reverential as the spirits could have wished.

Then there was Henry Sidgwick the philosopher, the last surviving representative of the Utilitarians. He had become a Fellow at a time when it was still necessary to sign the Thirty-Nine Articles, and he had signed them with full conscientious belief. Some years later he began to have doubts, and, although he was not required to sign the Articles again his conscience led him to resign his Fellowship. This action did much to hasten the abolition of this out-of-date requirement. In philosophical ability he was not quite in the first rank, but his intellectual integrity was absolute and undeviating. He married Arthur Balfour's sister, but did not agree with Arthur Balfour's politics. During the first months of the Boer War, he remarked that it would be very convenient for future schoolboys that the British Empire fell in exactly the year 1900. His lectures were not very interesting and those who listened to them came to know that there was always one joke. After the joke had come they let their attention wander. He had a stammer which he used very effectively. A German learned man once said to him. "You English have no word for *Gelehrte*." "Yes, we have," Sidgwick replied, "we call them p-p-p-p-prigs." I am sorry to say that there was a quarrel between him and another eminent man, Sir Richard Jebb, Professor of Greek and Member of Parliament for the university. A new road had to be made and part of Jebb's garden was cut off in order to make it. Sidgwick had agitated for the new road, which was needed to give access to Newham College, of which Mrs. Sidgwick was principal. This was bad enough. But when it was decided to call the road "Sidgwick Avenue" it was more than Jebb could bear. It was commonly said, though I do not vouch for the story, that Sidgwick remarked concerning Jebb, "All the time that he can spare from the adornment of his person, he devotes to the neglect of his duties." A slightly less bitter quarrel arose between Verrall and his neighbor James Ward the philosopher, because their wives agreed to share a pig tub and each said that the other contributed less than her moiety. But the quarrels were not very grave and contributed to everybody's entertainment. For James Ward, in spite of the affair of the pig tub, I had a profound respect and a considerable affection. He was my chief teacher in philosophy and, although afterward I came to disagree with him, I have remained grateful to him, not only for instruction, but for much kindness.

There were other Dons who interested me, although I knew them less well. Sir James Frazer, author of *The Golden Bough*, was one of these. Fellows had dinner in Hall without payment, and, as a Scot, Frazer could not ignore this consideration. Any Fellow arriving more than quarter of an hour late was subject to a fine, but Frazer grudged every minute taken from his studies for the gross work of self-nourishment. He therefore always arrived in Hall exactly quarter of an hour late. Then there was Sir George Darwin. Charles Darwin, his eminent father, had not been considered by the

University clever enough for a Honors degree and had contented himself with a Pass, but, since his time, intellectual standards in the university had deteriorated and his sons were allowed professorships. Sir George Darwin was famous as a mathematical physicist. One day when I went to lunch with him I found him and another famous mathematician, Sir Robert Ball, bending over a calculating machine which wouldn't work. After they had tinkered with it for a long time, Lady Darwin, who was American, came in and said, "All it wants is a little sewing-machine oil." And she was right.

One of the characteristics of academic personages was longevity. When I was a freshman, the College was dominated by three elderly dignitaries: the Master, the Vice-Master, and the Senior Fellow. When I returned to the College twenty years later as a lecturer, they were still going strong, and seemed no older. The Master had been Head Master of Harrow when my father was a boy there. I breakfasted at the Master's Lodge on a day which happened to be his sister-in-law's birthday, and when she came into the room he said, "Now, my dear, you have lasted just as long as the Peloponnesian War." The Vice-Master, who always stood as stiffly upright as a ramrod, never appeared out of doors except in a top hat, even when he was wakened by a fire at three in the morning. It was said that he never read a line of Tennyson after witnessing the poet putting water into the '34 port. Before dinner in Hall the Master and the Vice-Master used to read a long Latin Grace in alternate sentences. The Master adopted the Continental pronunciation but the Vice-Master adhered uncompromisingly to the old English style. The contrast was curious and enlivening. The Senior Fellow was the last survivor of the old system by which men got life Fellowships at twenty-two and had no further duties except to draw their dividend. This duty he performed punctiliously, but otherwise he was not known to have done any work whatever since the age of twenty-two.

As the case of the Senior Fellow shows, security of tenure was carried very far. The result was partly good, partly bad. Very good men flourished, and so did some who were not so good. Incompetence, oddity and even insanity were tolerated, but so was real merit. In spite of some lunacy and some laziness, Cambridge was a good place, where independence of mind could exist undeterred.

Some of My Contemporaries
at Cambridge

FROM the moment that I went up to Cambridge at the beginning of October 1890, everything went well with me. All the people then in residence who subsequently became my intimate friends called on me during the first week of term. At the time I did not know why they did so, but I discovered afterward that Whitehead, who had examined for scholarships, had told people to look out for Sanger and me. Sanger was a freshman like myself, also doing mathematics, and also a minor scholar. He and I both had rooms in Whewell's Court. Webb, our coach, had a practice of circulating MSS. among his classes, and it fell to my lot to deliver an MS. to Sanger after I had done with it. I had not seen him before, but I was struck by the books on his shelves. I said: "I see you have Draper's *Intellectual Development of Europe* which I think a very good book." He said: "You are the first person I have ever met who has heard of it!" From this point the conversation proceeded, and at the end of half an hour we were lifelong friends. We compared notes as to how much mathematics we had done. We agreed upon theology and metaphysics. We disagreed upon politics (he was at the time a Conservative, though in later life he belonged to the Labor Party). He spoke to me about Shaw, whose name was until then unknown to me. We used to work on mathematics together. He was incredibly quick, and would be halfway through solving a problem before I had understood the question. We both devoted our fourth year to moral science, but he did economics, and I did philosophy. We got our Fellowships at the same moment. He was one of the kindest men that ever lived, and in the last years of his life my children loved him as much as I have done. I have never known anyone else with such a perfect combination of penetrating intellect and warm affection. He became a Chancery barrister, and was known in legal circles for his highly erudite edition of Jarman *On Wills*. He was also a very good economist; and he could read an incredible number of languages, including such out-of-the-way items as Magyar and Finnish. I used to go on walking tours with him in Italy, and he always made me do all the conversation with innkeepers, but when I was reading Italian, I found that his knowledge of the language was vastly greater than mine. His death in the year 1930 was a great sorrow to me.

The other friends whom I acquired during my first term I owed chiefly to Whitehead's recommendation. Two of my closest friends were Crompton and Theodore Llewelyn Davies. Their father was vicar of Kirkby Lonsdale, and translator of Plato's *Republic* in the Golden Treasury edition, a distinguished scholar and a Broad Churchman whose views were derived from F. D. Maurice. He had a family of six sons and one daughter. It was said, and I believe with truth, that throughout their education the six sons, of whom Crompton and Theodore were the youngest, managed, by means of scholarships, to go through school and universtiy without expense to their father. Most of them were also strikingly good-looking, including Crompton, who had very fine blue eyes, which sometimes sparkled with fun and at other times had a steady gaze that was deeply serious. The ablest and one of the best loved of the family was the youngest, Theodore, with whom, when I first knew them, Crompton shared rooms in College. They both in due course became Fellows, but neither of them became resident. Afterward the two lived together in a small house near Westminster Abbey, in a quiet out-of-the-way street. Both of them were able, high-minded and passionate and shared, on the whole, the same ideals and opinions. Theodore had a somewhat more practical outlook on life than Crompton. He became private secretary to a series of Conservative Chancellors of the Exchequer, each of whom in turn he converted to Free Trade at a time when the rest of the Government wished them to think otherwise. He worked incredibly hard and yet always found time to give presents to the children of all his friends, and the presents were always exactly appropriate. He inspired the deepest affection in almost everybody who knew him. I never knew but one woman who would not have been delighted to marry him. She, of course, was the only woman he wished to marry. In the spring of 1905, when he was thirty-four, his dead body was found in a pool near Kirkby Lonsdale, where he had evidently bathed on his way to the station. It was supposed that he must have hit his head on a rock in diving.

One of my earliest memories of Crompton is of meeting him in the darkest part of a winding College staircase and his suddenly quoting, without any previous word, the whole of "Tyger, Tyger, burning bright." I had never, till that moment, heard of Blake, and the poem affected me so much that I became dizzy and had to lean against the wall.

What made Crompton at the same time so admirable and

so delightful was not his ability, but his strong loves and hates, his fantastic humor, and his rocklike honesty. He was one of the wittiest men that I have ever known, with a great love of mankind combined with a contemptuous hatred for most individual men. He had by no means the ways of a saint. Once, when we were both young, I was walking with him in the country, and we trespassed over a corner of a farmer's land. The farmer came running out after us, shouting and red with fury. Crompton held his hand to his ear, and said, with the utmost mildness: "Would you mind speaking a little louder? I'm rather hard of hearing." The farmer was reduced to speechlessness in the endeavor to make more noise than he was already making.

Crompton was addicted to extreme shabbiness in his clothes, to such a degree that some of his friends expostulated. This had an unexpected result. When West Australia attempted by litigation to secede from the Commonwealth of Australia, his law firm was employed, and it was decided that the case should be heard in the King's Robing Room. Crompton was overheard ringing up the King's Chamberlain and saying: "The unsatisfactory state of my trousers has lately been brought to my notice. I understand that the case is to be heard in the King's Robing Room. Perhaps the King has left an old pair of trousers there that might be useful to me."

Another friend of my Cambridge years was McTaggart, the philosopher, who was even shyer than I was. I heard a knock on my door one day—a very gentle knock. I said, "Come in," but nothing happened. I said "Come in," louder. The door opened and I saw McTaggart standing on the mat. He was already President of The Union, and about to become a Fellow, and inspired me with awe on account of his metaphysical reputation, but he was too shy to come in, and I was too shy to ask him to come in. I cannot remember how many minutes this situation lasted, but somehow or other he was at last in the room. After that I used frequently to go to his breakfasts, which were famous for their lack of food; in fact, anybody who had been once, brought an egg with him on every subsequent occasion. McTaggart was a Hegelian, and at that time still young and enthusiastic. He had a great intellectual influence upon my generation, though in retrospect I do not think it was a very good one. For two or three years, under his influence, I was a Hegelian. Although after 1898 I no longer accepted McTaggart's philosophy, I remained fond of him until an occasion during the First War, when he asked me no longer to come and see him because he could not bear my opinions. He followed this up by taking a leading part in having me turned out of my lectureship.

Two other friends whom I met in my early days in Cambridge and retained ever since, were Lowes Dickinson and Roger Fry. Dickinson was a man who inspired affection by his gentleness and pathos. When he was a Fellow and I was still an undergraduate, I became aware that I was liable to hurt him by my somewhat brutal statement of unpleasant truths, or what I thought to be such. States of the world which made me caustic only made him sad, and to the end of his days whenever I met him, I was afraid of increasing his unhappiness by too stark a realism. But perhaps realism is not quite the right word. What I really mean is the practice of describing things which one finds almost unendurable in such a repulsive manner as to cause others to share one's fury. He told me once that I resembled Cordelia, but it cannot be said that he resembled King Lear.

For a long time I supposed that somewhere in the University there were really clever people whom I had not yet met, and whom I should at once recognize as my intellectual superiors, but during my second year I discovered that I already knew all the cleverest people in the university. This was a disappointment to me. In my third year, however, I met G. E. Moore, who was then a freshman, and for some years he fulfilled my ideal of genius. He was in those days beautiful and slim, with a look almost of inspiration, and with an intellect as deeply passionate as Spinoza's. He had a kind of exquisite purity. I have never but once succeeded in making him tell a lie, and that was by a subterfuge. "Moore," I said, "do you *always* speak the truth?" "No," he replied. I believe this to be the only lie he has ever told.

Moore, like me, was influenced by McTaggart, and was for a short time a Hegelian. But he emerged more quickly than I did, and it was largely his conversation that led me to abandon both Kant and Hegel. In spite of his being two years younger than I, he greatly influenced my philosophical outlook. One of the pet amusements of all Moore's friends was to watch him trying to light a pipe. He would light a match, and then begin to argue, and continue until the match burned his fingers. Then he would light another, and so on, until the box was finished. This was no doubt fortunate for his health, as it provided moments during which he was not smoking.

Then there were the three brothers Trevelyan. Charles was the eldest. Bob, the second, was my special friend. He became a very scholarly poet. When he was young he had a delicious whimsical humor. Once, when we were on a reading party in the Lake District, Eddie Marsh, having overslept himself, came down in his nightshirt to see if breakfast was ready, looking frozen and miserable. Bob christened him "Cold white shape," and this name stuck to him for a long time. George Trevelyan was considerably younger than Bob, but I got to know him well later on. He and Charles were terrific walkers. Once when I went on a walking tour with

George in Devonshire, I made him promise to be content with twenty-five miles a day. He kept his promise. But at the end of the last day he left me, saying that now he must have a little walking.

Bob Trevelyan was, I think, the most bookish person that I have ever known. What is in books appeared to him interesting, whereas what is only real life was negligible. Like all the family, he had a minute knowledge of the strategy and tactics concerned in all the great battles of the world, so far as these appear in reputable books of history. But I was staying with him during the crisis of the Battle of the Marne, and as it was Sunday we could only get a newspaper by walking two miles. He did not think the battle sufficiently interesting to be worth it, because battles in mere newspapers are vulgar. I once devised a test question which I put to many people to discover whether they were pessimists. The question was: "If you had the power to destroy the world, would you do so?" I put the question to him, and he replied: "What? Destroy my library? —Never!" He was always discovering new poets and reading their poems out aloud, but he always began deprecatingly: "This is not one of his best poems." Once when he mentioned a new poet to me, and said he would like to read me some of his things, I said: "Yes, but don't read me a poem which is not one of his best." This stumped him completely, and he put the volume away.

I have not time to tell of many others who were important to me. Eddie Marsh (afterward Sir Edward) was my close friend. So was Desmond MacCarthy. E. M. Forster and Lytton Strachey and Keynes I knew well, though they were considerably junior to me. As a set, we were earnest, hardworking and intellectually adventurous. In spite of rather solemn ambitions, we had lots of fun and thoroughly enjoyed life, and we never got in the way of each other's individualities. We formed friendships that remained important through life, and a surprising number of us remained true to our early beliefs. It was a generation that I am glad to have belonged to.

George Bernard Shaw

BERNARD SHAW's long life could be divided into three phases. In the first, which lasted till he was about forty, he was known to a fairly wide circle as a musical critic, and to a much more restricted circle as a Fabian controversialist, an admirable novelist, and a dangerously witty enemy of humbug. Then came his second phase, as a writer of comedies. At first he could not get his plays performed, because they were not exactly like those of Pinero, but at last even theatrical managers realized that they were amusing, and he achieved a very well-deserved success. He had, I believe, cherished throughout his earlier life the hope that, when he had acquired an audience as a joker, he would be able effectively to deliver his serious message. Accordingly, in his third and last phase, he appeared as a prophet demanding equal admiration for St. Joan of Orleans and St. Joseph of Moscow. I knew him in all three phases, and in his first two I thought him both delightful and useful. In his third phase, however, I found that my admiration had limits.

I heard of him first in 1890, when I, as a freshman, met another freshman who admired his *Quintessence of Ibsenism*, but I did not meet him until 1896 when he took part in an International Socialist Congress in London. I knew a great many of the German delegates, as I had been studying German Social Democracy. They regarded Shaw as an incarnation of Satan, because he could not resist the pleasure of fanning the flames whenever there was a dispute. I, however, derived my view of him from the Webbs, and admired his Fabian essay in which he set to work to lead British Socialism away from Marx. He was at this time still shy. Indeed, I think that his wit, like that of many famous humorists, was developed as a defense against expected hostile ridicule. At this time he was just beginning to write plays, and he came to my flat to read one of them to a small gathering of friends. He was white and trembling with nervousness, and not at all the formidable figure that he became later. Shortly afterward, he and I stayed with the Webbs in Monmouthshire while he was learning the technique of the drama. He would write the names of all his characters on little squares of paper, and, when he was doing a scene, he would put on a chess board in front of him the names of the characters who were on the stage in that scene.

At this time he and I were involved in a bicycle accident, which I feared for a moment might have brought his career to a premature close. He was only just learning to ride a bicycle, and he ran into my machine with such force that he was hurled through the air and landed on his back twenty feet from the place of the collision. However, he got up completely unhurt and continued his ride; whereas my bicycle was smashed, and I had to return by train. It was a very slow train, and at every station Shaw with his bicycle appeared on the platform, put his head into the carriage and jeered. I suspect that he regarded the whole incident as proof of the virtues of vegetarianism.

Lunching with Mr. and Mrs. Shaw in Adelphi Terrace was a somewhat curious experience. Mrs. Shaw was a very able manager and used to provide Shaw with such a delicious vegetarian meal that the guests all regretted their more conventional menu. But he could not resist a somewhat frequent repetition of his favorite anecdotes. Whenever he came to his uncle who committed suicide by putting his head in a carpet-bag and then shutting it, a look of unutterable boredom used to appear on Mrs. Shaw's face, and if one were sitting next her one had to take care not to listen to Shaw. This, however, did not prevent her from solicitude for him. I remember a luncheon at which a young and lovely poetess was present in the hopes of reading her poems to Shaw. As we said good-by, Shaw informed us that she was staying behind for this purpose. Nevertheless, when we departed we found her on the mat, Mrs. Shaw having maneuvered her there by methods that I was not privileged to observe. When I learned, not long afterward, that this same lady had cut her throat at Wells because he refused to make love to her, I conceived an even higher respect than before for Mrs. Shaw.

Wifely solicitude toward Shaw was no sinecure. When they and the Webbs were all nearing eighty, they came to see me at my house on the South Downs. The house had a tower from which there was a very fine view, and all of them climbed the stairs. Shaw was first and Mrs. Shaw last. All the time that he was climbing, her voice came up from below, calling out, "GBS, don't talk while you're going up the stairs!" But her advice was totally ineffective, and his sentences flowed on quite uninterruptedly.

Shaw's attack on Victorian humbug and hypocrisy was as beneficent as it was delightful, and for this the English undoubtedly owe him a debt of gratitude. It was a part of Victorian humbug to endeavor to conceal vanity. When I was young, we all made a show of thinking no better of ourselves than of our neighbors. Shaw found this effort wearisome, and had already given it up when he first burst upon the world. It used to be the custom among clever people to say that Shaw was not unusually vain, but only unusually candid. I came to think later on that this was a mistake. Two incidents at which I was present convinced me of this. The first was a luncheon in London in honor of Bergson, to which Shaw had been invited as an admirer, along with a number of professional philosophers whose attitude to Bergson was more critical. Shaw set to work to expound Bergson's philosophy in the style of the preface to *Methuselah*. In this version, the philosophy was hardly one to recommend itself to professionals, and Bergson mildly interjected, "Ah, no-o! it is not qvite zat!" But Shaw was quite unabashed, and replied, "Oh, my dear fellow, I understand your philosophy much better than you do." Bergson clenched his fists and nearly exploded with rage; but, with a great effort, he controlled himself, and Shaw's expository monologue continued.

The second incident was an encounter with the elder Masaryk, who was in London officially, and intimated through his secretary that there were certain people whom he would like to see at 10:00 A.M. before his official duties began. I was one of them, and when I arrived I discovered that the only others were Shaw and Wells and Swinnerton. The rest of us arrived punctually, but Shaw was late. He marched straight up to the Great Man and said: "Masaryk, the foreign policy of Czechoslovakia is all wrong." He expounded this theme for about ten minutes, and left without waiting to hear Masaryk's reply.

Shaw, like many witty men, considered wit an adequate substitute for wisdom. He could defend any idea, however silly, so cleverly as to make those who did not accept it look like fools. I met him once at an "Erewhon Dinner" in honor of Samuel Butler and I learned with surprise that he accepted as gospel every word uttered by that sage, and even theories that were only intended as jokes, as, for example, that the Odyssey was written by a woman. Butler's influence on Shaw was much greater than most people realized. It was from him that Shaw acquired his antipathy to Darwin, which afterward made him an admirer of Bergson. It is a curious fact that the views which Butler adopted, in order to have an excuse for quarreling with Darwin, became part of officially enforced orthodoxy in the U.S.S.R.

Shaw's contempt for science was indefensible. Like Tolstoy, he couldn't believe in the importance of anything he didn't know. He was passionate against vivisection. I think the reason was, not any sympathy for animals, but a disbelief in the scientific knowledge which vivisection is held to provide. His vegetarianism also, I think, was not due to humanitarian motives, but rather to his ascetic impulses, to which he gave full expression in the last act of *Methuselah*.

Shaw was at his best as a controversialist. If there was anything silly or anything insincere about his opponent, Shaw would seize on it unerringly to the delight of all those who were on his side in the controversy. At the beginning of the First World War he published his *Common Sense about the War*. Although he did not write as a Pacifist, he infuriated most patriotic people by refusing to acquiesce in the hypocritical high moral tone of the Government and its followers. He was entirely praiseworthy in this sort of way, until he fell a victim to adulation of the Soviet Government and suddenly lost the power of criticism and of seeing through humbug if it came from Moscow. Excellent as he was in controversy, he was not nearly so good when it came to setting forth his own opinions, which were somewhat chaotic until in his last years he acquiesced in systematic Marxism. Shaw had many qualities which deserve great admiration. He was completely fearless. He expressed his opinions with equal vigor whether they were popular or unpopular. He was merciless toward those who deserve no mercy—but sometimes, also, to those who did not deserve to be his victims. In sum, one may say that he did much good and some harm. As an iconoclast he was admirable, but as an icon rather less so.

H. G. Wells

I FIRST met H. G. Wells in 1902 at a small discussion society created by Sidney Webb and by him christened "The Co-efficients" in the hope that we should be jointly efficient. There were about a dozen of us. Some have escaped my memory. Among those whom I remember, the most distinguished was Sir Edward Grey. Then there was H. J. MacKinder (afterward Sir) who was Reader in Geography at the University of Oxford and a great authority on the then new German subject of geopolitics. What I found most interesting about him was that he had climbed Kilimanjaro with a native guide who walked barefoot except in villages, where he wore dancing pumps. There was Amory. And there was Commander Bellairs, a breezy naval officer who was engaged in a perpetual dingdong battle for the Parliamentary representation of Kings Lynn with an opponent universally known as Tommy Bowles, a gallant champion of the army. Commander Bellairs was a Liberal and Tommy Bowles a Conservative; but, after a while, Commander Bellairs became a Conservative, and Tommy Bowles became a Liberal. They were thus enabled to continue their duel at Kings Lynn. In 1902 Commander Bellairs was halfway on the journey from the old party to the new one. And there was

W. A. S. Hewins, the director of the School of Economics. Hewins once told me that he had been brought up a Roman Catholic, but had since replaced faith in the Church by faith in the British Empire. He was passionately opposed to Free Trade, and was successfully engaged in converting Joseph Chamberlain to Tariff Reform. I know how large a part he had in this conversion, as he showed me the correspondence between himself and Chamberlain before Chamberlain had come out publicly for Tariff Reform.

I had never heard of Wells until Webb mentioned him as a man whom he had invited to become a Co-efficient. Webb informed me that Wells was a young man who, for the moment, wrote stories in the style of Jules Verne, but hoped, when these made his name and fortune, to devote himself to more serious work. I very soon found that I was too much out of sympathy with most of the Co-efficients to be able to profit by the discussions or contribute usefully to them. All the members except Wells and myself were Imperialists and looked forward without too much apprehension to a war with Germany. I was drawn to Wells by our common antipathy to this point of view. He was a Socialist, and at that time, though not later, considered great wars a folly. Matters came to a head when Sir Edward Grey, then in Opposition, advocated what became the policy of the Entente with France and Russia, which was adopted by the Conservative Government some two years later, and solidified by Sir Edward Grey when he became Foreign Secretary. I spoke vehemently against this policy, which I felt led straight to world war, but no one except Wells agreed with me.

As a result of the political sympathy between us, I invited Wells and Mrs. Wells to visit me at Bagley Wood, near Oxford, where I then lived. The visit was not altogether a success. Wells, in our presence, accused Mrs. Wells of a Cockney accent, an accusation which (so it seemed to me) could more justly be brought against him. More serious was a matter arising out of a book that he had lately written called *In the Days of the Comet*. In this book the earth passes through the tail of a comet which contains a gas that makes everybody sensible. The victory of good sense is shown in two ways: a war between England and Germany, which had been raging, is stopped by mutual consent; and everybody takes to free love. Wells was assailed in the Press, not for his pacifism, but for his advocacy of free love. He replied somewhat heatedly that he had not advocated free love, but had merely prophesied possible effects of new ingredients in the atmosphere without saying whether he thought these effects good or bad. This seemed to me disingenuous, and I asked him, "Why did you first advocate free love and then say you hadn't?" He replied that he had not yet saved enough money out of royalties to be able to live on the interest, and that he did not propose to advocate free love publicly until he had done so. I was in those days perhaps unduly strict, and this answer displeased me.

After this I did not see much of him until the First World War had ended. In spite of his previous attitude about war with Germany, he became exceedingly bellicose in 1914. He invented the phrase about "a war to end war." He said that he was "enthusiastic for this war against Prussian militarism." In the very first days, he stated that the whole Prussian military machine was paralyzed before the defenses of Liège—which fell a day or two later. Sidney Webb, although he agreed with Wells about the war, had ceased to be on good terms with him, partly from moral disapproval, partly because Wells undertook an elaborate campaign to win from Webb the leadership of the Fabian Society. Wells's hostility to the Webbs was expressed in several novels, and was never appeased.

After the end of the first war, my relations with Wells became again more friendly. I admired his *Outline of History*, especially its earlier parts, and found myself in agreement with his opinions on a great many subjects. He had immense energy and a capacity to organize great masses of material. He was also a very vivacious and amusing talker. His eyes were very bright, and in an argument one felt that he was taking an impersonal interest in the subject rather than a personal interest in his interlocutor. I used to visit him at weekends at his house in Essex where, on Sunday afternoons, he would take his house party to visit his neighbor Lady Warwick. She was an active supporter of the Labor Party, and her park contained a lake surrounded by huge green porcelain frogs given her by Edward VII. It was a little difficult to adapt one's conversation to both these aspects of her personality.

Wells derived his importance from quantity rather than quality, though one must admit that he excelled in certain qualities. He was very good at imagining mass behavior in unusual circumstances, for example in *The War of the Worlds*. Some of his novels depict convincingly heroes not unlike himself. Politically, he was one of those who made Socialism respectable in England. He had a very considerable influence upon the generation that followed him, not only as regards politics but also as regards matters of personal ethics. His knowledge, though nowhere profound, was very extensive. He had, however, certain weaknesses which somewhat interfered with his position as a sage. He found unpopularity very hard to endure, and would make concessions to popular clamor which interfered with the consistency of his teaching. He had a sympathy with the masses which made him liable to share their occasional hysterias. When he was worried by accusations of immorality or infidelity, he would write somewhat second-rate stories designed to rebut such charges, such as *The Soul of a Bishop* or the story of the husband and wife who are beginning to quarrel and, to stop this process, spend the winter in Labrador and are reconciled by a common fight against a bear. The last time I saw him, which was shortly before his death, he spoke with great earnestness of the harm done by divisions on the Left, and I gathered, though he did not explicitly say so, that he thought Socialists ought to co-operate with Communists more than they were doing. This had not been his view in the heyday of his vigor, when he used to make fun of Marx's beard and exhort people not to adopt the new Marxist orthodoxy.

Wells's importance was primarily as a liberator of thought and imagination. He was able to construct pictures of possible societies, both attractive and unattractive, of a sort that encouraged the young to envisage possibilities which otherwise they would not have thought of. Sometimes he does this in a very illuminating way. His *Country of the Blind* is a somewhat pessimistic restatement in modern language of Plato's allegory of the cave. His various utopias, though perhaps not in themselves very solid, are calculated to start trains of thought which may prove fruitful. He is always rational, and avoids various forms of superstition to which modern minds are prone. His belief in scientific method is healthful and invigorating. His general optimism, although the state of the world makes it difficult to sustain, is much more likely to lead to good results than the somewhat lazy pessimism which is becoming all too common. In spite of some reservations, I think one should regard Wells as having been an important force toward sane and constructive thinking both as regards social systems and as regards personal relations. I hope he may have successors, though I do not at the moment know who they will be.

Joseph Conrad

I MADE the acquaintance of Joseph Conrad in September 1913, through our common friend Lady Ottoline Morrell. I had been for many years an admirer of his books, but should not have ventured to seek acquaintance without an introduction. I traveled down to his house near Ashford in Kent in a state of somewhat anxious expectation. My first impression was one of surprise. He spoke English with a very strong foreign accent, and nothing in his demeanor in any way suggested the sea. He was an aristocratic Polish gentleman to his finger tips. His feeling for the sea, and for England, was one of romantic love—love from a certain distance, sufficient to leave the romance untarnished. His love for the sea began at a very early age. When he told his parents that he wished for a career as a sailor, they urged him to go into the Austrian navy, but he wanted adventure and tropical seas and strange rivers surrounded by dark forests; and the Austrian navy offered him no scope for these desires. His family were horrified at his seeking a career in the English merchant marine, but his determination was inflexible.

He was, as anyone may see from his books, a very rigid moralist and politically far from sympathetic with revolutionaries. He and I were in most of our opinions by no means in agreement, but in something very fundamental we were extraordinarily at one.

My relation to Joseph Conrad was unlike any other that I have ever had. I saw him seldom, and not over a long period of years. In the outworks of our lives, we were almost strangers, but we shared a certain outlook on human life and human destiny, which, from the very first, made a bond of extreme strength. I may perhaps be pardoned for quoting a sentence from a letter that he wrote to me very soon after we had become acquainted. I should feel that modesty forbids the quotation except for the fact that it expresses so exactly what I felt about him. What he expressed and I equally felt was, in his words, "A deep admiring affection which, if you were never to see me again and forgot my existence tomorrow, would be unalterably yours *usque ad finem.*"

Of all that he had written I admired most the terrible story called *The Heart of Darkness*, in which a rather weak idealist is driven mad by horror of the tropical forest and loneliness among savages. This story expresses, I think, most completely his philosophy of life. I felt, though I do not know whether he would have accepted such an image, that he thought of civilized and morally tolerable human life as a dangerous walk on a thin crust of barely cooled lava which at any moment might break and let the unwary sink into fiery depths. He was very conscious of the various forms of passionate madness to which men are prone, and it was this that gave him such a profound belief in the importance of discipline. His point of view, one might perhaps say, was the antithesis of Rousseau's: "Man is born in chains, but he can become free." He becomes free, so I believe Conrad would have said, not by letting loose his impulses, not by being casual and uncontrolled, but by subduing wayward impulse to a dominant purpose.

He was not much interested in political systems, though he had some strong political *feelings*. The strongest of these were love of England and hatred of Russia, of which both are expressed in *The Secret Agent:* and the hatred of Russia, both Czarist and revolutionary, is set forth with great power in *Under Western Eyes*. His dislike of Russia was that which was traditional in Poland. It went so far that he would not allow merit to either Tolstoy or Dostoievsky. Turgeniev, he told me once, was the only Russian novelist he admired.

Except for love of England and hatred of Russia, politics did not much concern him. What interested him was the individual human soul faced with the indifference of nature, and often with the hostility of man, and subject to inner struggles with passions both good and bad that led toward destruction. Tragedies of loneliness occupied a great part of his thought and feeling. One of his most typical stories is *Typhoon*. In this story the captain, who is a simple soul, pulls his ship through by unshakable courage and grim determination. When the storm is over, he writes a long letter to his wife telling about it. In his account his own part is, to him, perfectly simple. He has merely performed his captain's duty as, of course, anyone would expect. But the reader, through his narrative, becomes aware of all that he has done and dared and endured. The letter, before he sends it off, is read surreptitiously by his steward, but is never read by anyone else at all because his wife finds it boring and throws it away unread.

The two things that seem most to occupy Conrad's imagination are loneliness and fear of what is strange. *An Outcast of the Islands* like *The Heart of Darkness* is concerned with fear of what is strange. Both come together in the extraordinarily moving story called *Amy Foster*. In this story a South-Slav peasant, on his way to America, is the sole survivor of the wreck of his ship, and is cast away in a Kentish village.

All the village fears and ill treats him, except Amy Foster, a dull, plain girl who brings him bread when he is starving and finally marries him. But she, too, when, in fever, her husband reverts to his native language, is seized with a fear of his strangeness, snatches up their child and abandons him. He dies alone and hopeless. I have wondered at times how much of this man's loneliness Conrad had felt among the English and had suppressed by a stern effort of will.

Conrad's point of view was far from modern. In the modern world there are two philosophies: the one, which stems from Rousseau, and sweeps aside discipline as unnecessary; the other, which finds its fullest expression in totalitarianism, which thinks of discipline as essentially imposed from without. Conrad adhered to the older tradition, that discipline should come from within. He despised indiscipline, and hated discipline that was merely external.

In all this I found myself closely in agreement with him. At our very first meeting, we talked with continually increasing intimacy. We seemed to sink through layer after layer of what was superficial, till gradually both reached the central fire. It was an experience unlike any other that I have known. We looked into each other's eyes, half appalled and half intoxicated to find ourselves together in such a region. The emotion was as intense as passionate love, and at the same time all-embracing. I came away bewildered, and hardly able to find my way among ordinary affairs.

I saw nothing of Conrad during the war or after it until my return from China in 1921. When my first son was born in that year I wished Conrad to be as nearly his godfather as was possible without a formal ceremony. I wrote to Conrad saying: "I wish, with your permission, to call my son John Conrad. My father was called John, my grandfather was called John, and my great-grandfather was called John; and

Conrad is a name in which I see merits." He accepted the position and duly presented my son with the cup which is usual on such occasions.

I did not see much of him, as I lived most of the year in Cornwall, and his health was failing. But I had some charming letters from him, especially one about my book on China. He wrote: "I have always liked the Chinese, even those that tried to kill me (and some other people) in the yard of a private house in Chantabun, even (but not so much) the fellow who stole all my money one night in Bangkok, but brushed and folded my clothes neatly for me to dress in the morning, before vanishing into the depths of Siam. I also received many kindnesses at the hands of various Chinese. This with the addition of an evening's conversation with the secretary of His Excellency Tseng on the verandah of a hotel and a perfunctory study of a poem, 'The Heathen Chinee' is all I know about Chinese. But after reading your extremely interesting view of the Chinese Problem I take a gloomy view of the future of their country." He went on to say that my views of the future of China "strike a chill into one's soul," the more so, he said, as I pinned my hopes on international socialism— "The sort of thing," he commented, "to which I cannot attach any sort of definite meaning. I have never been able to find in any man's book or any man's talk anything convincing enough to stand up for a moment against my deep-seated sense of fatality governing this man-inhabited world." He went on to say that although man has taken to flying, "He doesn't fly like an eagle, he flies like a beetle. And you must have noticed how ugly, ridiculous and fatuous is the flight of a beetle." In these pessimistic remarks, I felt that he was showing a deeper wisdom than I had shown in my somewhat artificial hopes for a happy issue in China. It must be said that so far events have proved him right.

This letter was my last contact with him. I never again saw him to speak to. Once I saw him across the street, in earnest conversation with a man I did not know, standing outside the door of what had been my grandmother's house, but after her death had become the Arts Club. I did not like to interrupt what seemed a serious conversation, and I went away. When he died, shortly afterward, I was sorry I had not been bolder. The house is gone, demolished by Hitler. Conrad, I suppose, is in process of being forgotten. But his intense and passionate nobility shines in my memory like a star seen from the bottom of a well. I wish I could make his light shine for others as it shone for me.

George Santayana

I FIRST met Santayana on a roof in Temple Gardens one very warm evening in June 1893. After a day of sweltering heat, the temperature had become delicious and the view of London was intoxicating. I had just finished the Mathematical Tripos after ten years of arduous preparation and was about to embark on the study of philosophy. My brother, through whom I came to know Santayana, informed me that he was a philosopher. I therefore looked upon him with great reverence, all the more so as my mood was one of expansive liberation. He had at that time large lustrous eyes of considerable beauty. I listened to him with respect, since he seemed to embody a difficult synthesis, namely, that of America and Spain. I cannot, however, remember anything of his conversation on that occasion.

As I came to know him better I found some sympathy and much divergence. He professed a certain detachment which was not wholly sincere. Although both his parents were Spanish, he had been brought up in Boston and taught philosophy at Harvard. Nevertheless he felt himself always an exile from Spain. In the Spanish-American War he found himself passionately on the Spanish side, which is perhaps not surprising, as his father had been Governor of Manila. Whenever his

Spanish patriotism was involved, his usual air of detachment disappeared. He used to spend the summers at his sister's house in the ancient city of Avila, and he described to me once how the ladies there would sit at their windows, flirting with such male acquaintances as passed by, and would make up for this pastime afterward by going to confession. I rashly remarked: "It sounds a rather vapid existence." He drew himself up, and replied sharply: "They spend their lives in the two greatest things: love and religion."

He could admit into the realms of his admirations the ancient Greeks and the modern Italians, even Mussolini. But he could feel no sincere respect for anyone who came from north of the Alps. He held that only the Mediterranean peoples are capable of contemplation, and that therefore they alone can be true philosophers. German and British philosophies he regarded as the stumbling efforts of immature races. He liked, in northern countries, athletes and men of affairs. He was a close friend of my brother, who made no rash attempts to penetrate the arcana. But toward me, as toward other northern philosophers, his attitude was one of gentle pity for having attempted something too high for us. This, however, never interfered with pleasant relations, as my patriotic self-confidence was quite equal to his.

Santayana in private life was very similar to what he was in his books. He was suave, meticulous in his ways, and very seldom excited. A few days before the Battle of the Marne, when the capture of Paris by the Germans seemed imminent, he remarked to me: "I think I must go to Paris, because my winter underclothes are there, and I should not like the Germans to get them. I have also left there the manuscript of a book on which I have been working for the last ten years; but I don't mind so much about that." However, the Battle of the Marne obviated the necessity of this journey.

One evening in Cambridge, after I had been seeing him every day for some time, he remarked to me: "I am going to Seville tomorrow. I wish to be in a place where people do not restrain their passions." I suppose this attitude is not surprising in one who had few passions to restrain.

He relates in his autobiography one occasion when my brother succeeded in rousing him to a certain warmth of feeling. My brother had a yacht on which Santayana was to accompany him. The yacht was moored and could only be approached by a very narrow plank. My brother ran lightly across it, but Santayana was afraid of falling into the mud. My brother reached out a hand to him, but unfortunately Santayana's balance was so bad that both fell with a splash into the semiliquid mire of the river bank. Santayana relates with some horror that on this occasion my brother used words which he would not have expected an earl to know.

There was always something rather prim about Santayana. His clothes were always neat, and even in country lanes he wore patent-leather button boots. I think a person of sufficient intelligence might perhaps have guessed these characteristics from his literary style.

Although not a believing Catholic, he strongly favored the Catholic religion in all political and social ways. He did not see any reason to wish that the populace should believe something true. What he desired for the populace was some myth to which he could give aesthetic approval. This attitude naturally made him very hostile to Protestantism, and made people with a Protestant way of feeling critical of him. William James condemned his doctor's thesis as "the perfection of rottenness." And, although the two men were colleagues for a great many years, neither ever succeeded in thinking well of the other.

For my part, I was never able to take Santayana very seri-

ously as a technical philosopher, although I thought that he
served a useful function by bringing to bear, as a critic, points
of view which are now uncommon. The American dress in
which his writing appeared somewhat concealed the extremely reactionary character of his thinking. Not only did
he, as a Spaniard, side politically with the Church in all its attempts to bolster up old traditions in that country, but, as a
philosopher, he reverted in great measure to the scholasticism
of the thirteenth century. He did not present this doctrine
straightforwardly as neo-Thomists do; he insinuated it under
various aliases, so that it was easy for a reader not to know
where his opinions came from. It would not be fair to suggest
that his views were completely those of medieval scholastics.
He took rather more from Plato than St. Thomas did. But I
think that he and St. Thomas, if they could have met, would
have understood each other very well.

His two chief works in pure philosophy were *The Life of
Reason*, published in 1905, and *Realms of Being*, published
between 1927 and 1940. He deals with the life of reason under five headings: reason in common sense, in society, in religion, in art, and in science. I do not myself feel that this work
is very likely to attract a reader to the sort of life which Santayana considers rational. It is too quiet, too much that of a
mere spectator, too destitute of passion, which, though it may
have to be controlled, seems, to me at least, an essential element in any life worth living. His *Realms of Being*, which
was his last important philosophical work, deals successively
with essence, matter, truth, and spirit. In this, as in his other
philosophical books, he does not trouble to argue, and much
of what he says, particularly as regards essence, ignores much
work which most modern philosophers would consider relevant. He completely ignored modern logic, which has thrown
much new light on the old problem of universals which oc-

cupied a very large part of the attention of the scholastics. Santayana's *Realm of Essence* seems to presuppose, at any rate in some sense, the reality of universals. It would be rash to say that this doctrine is false, but it is characteristic of Santayana that he calmly assumes its truth without taking the trouble to offer any arguments in its favor.

Although most of his active life was spent as a professor of philosophy at Harvard, he was perhaps more important from a literary than from a philosophic point of view. His style, to my mind, is not quite what a style ought to be. Like his patent-leather boots, it is too smooth and polished. The impression one gets in reading him is that of floating down a smooth-flowing river, so broad that you can seldom see either bank; but, when from time to time a promontory comes into view, you are surprised that it is a new one, as you have been unconscious of movement. I find myself, in reading him, approving each sentence in an almost somnambulistic manner, but quite unable, after a few pages, to remember what it was all about.

Nevertheless, I owe him certain philosophical debts. When I was young, I agreed with G. E. Moore in believing in the objectivity of good and evil. Santayana's criticism, in a book called *Winds of Doctrine*, caused me to abandon this view, though I have never been able to be as bland and comfortable without it as he was.

He wrote a good deal of literary criticism, some of it excellent. There was a book called *Three Philosophical Poets* about Lucretius, Dante, and Goethe. He was rather hurt because I said that he was better about the two Italian poets than about the German one. His writing on Goethe seemed to me a *tour de force* in which his intellectual approval was continually at war with his temperamental disgust. I found the latter more interesting than the former, and wished he had given it free rein.

He had a considerable affection for England, and his *Soliloquies in England* is a book which any patriotic English person can read with pleasure. He wrote a novel in which my brother (for whom he had a considerable affection) appears as the villain. He wrote an autobiography in several parts, which is chiefly interesting as exhibiting the clash between his Spanish temperament and his Boston environment. He used to boast that his mother, as a widow in Boston, worried her New England friends by never being busy about anything; and, when they came on a deputation to ask her how she got through the time, she replied : "Well, I'll tell you. In summer I try to keep cool, and in winter I try to keep warm." Admiration for this answer prevented him from feeling at home in New England.

He wrote a great deal about American culture, of which he had no high opinion. He gave an address to the University of California called *The Genteel Tradition in American Philosophy*, the gist of which was to the effect that academic America is alien to the spirit of the country, which, he said, is vigorous but Philistine. It had seemed to me, in my wanderings through American universities, that they would be more in harmony with the spirit of the country if they were housed in skyscrapers and not in pseudo-Gothic buildings ranged round a campus. This was also Santayana's view. I felt, however, a certain difference. Santayana enjoyed being aloof and contemptuous, whereas I found this attitude, when forced upon me, extremely painful. Aloofness and facile contempt were his defects, and because of them, although he could be admired, he was a person whom it was difficult to love.

But it is only fair to counterbalance this judgment with his judgment of me. He says: "Even when Russell's insight is keenest, the very intensity of his vision concentrates it too much. The focus is microscopic; he sees one thing at a time with extraordinary clearness, or one strain in history or politics; and the vivid realization of that element blinds him to the rest." And he accuses me, oddly enough, of religious conservatism. I will leave the reader to form his own judgment on this matter.

Santayana never seems to have felt that his loyalty to the past, if he could have caused it to become general, would have produced a lifeless world in which no new good thing could grow up. If he had lived in the time of Galileo he would have pointed out the literary inferiority of Galileo to Lucretius. But Lucretius was setting forth a doctrine already several centuries old, and I doubt whether the works of Democritus and Epicurus which set forth the doctrine when it was new, were as aesthetically pleasing as the poem of Lucretius. But, perhaps fortunately for them, their works are lost and my opinion can be no more than a guess. What remains indubitable is that the new is never as mellow as the old, and that therefore the worship of mellowness is incompatible with new excellence. It is for this reason that Santayana's merits are literary rather than philosophical.

Alfred North Whitehead

M Y FIRST contact with Whitehead, or rather with his father, was in 1877. I had been told that the earth is round, but trusting to the evidence of the senses, I refused to believe it. The vicar of the parish, who happened to be Whitehead's father, was called in to persuade me. Clerical authority so far prevailed as to make me think an experimental test worth while, and I started to dig a hole in the hopes of emerging at the antipodes. When they told me this was useless, my doubts revived.

I had no further contact with Whitehead until the year 1890 when as a freshman at Cambridge, I attended his lectures on statics. He told the class to study article 35 in the textbook. Then he turned to me and said, "You needn't study it, because you know it already." I had quoted it by number in the scholarship examination ten months earlier. He won my heart by remembering this fact. His kindness did not end there. On the basis of the scholarship examination he told all the cleverest undergraduates to look out for me, so that within a week I had made the acquaintance of all of them and many of them became my lifelong friends.

Throughout the gradual transition from a student to an independent writer, I profited by Whitehead's guidance. The turning point was my Fellowship dissertation in 1895. I went to see him the day before the result was announced and he criticized my work somewhat severely, though quite justly. I was very crestfallen and decided to go away from Cambridge without waiting for the announcement next day. (I changed my mind, however, when James Ward praised my dissertation.) After I knew that I had been elected to a Fellowship, Mrs. Whitehead took him to task for the severity of his criticism, but he defended himself by saying that it was the last time that he would be able to speak to me as a pupil. When, in 1900, I began to have ideas of my own, I had the good fortune to persuade him that they were not without value. This was the basis of our ten years' collaboration on a big book no part of which is wholly due to either.

In England, Whitehead was regarded only as a mathematician, and it was left to America to discover him as a philosopher. He and I disagreed in philosophy, so that collaboration was no longer possible, and after he went to America I naturally saw much less of him. We began to drift apart during the First World War when he completely disagreed with my Pacifist position. In our differences on this subject he was more tolerant than I was, and it was much more my fault than his that these differences caused a diminution in the closeness of our friendship.

In the last months of the war his younger son, who was only just eighteen, was killed. This was an appalling grief to him, and it was only by an immense effort of moral discipline that he was able to go on with his work. The pain of this loss had a great deal to do with turning his thoughts to philosophy and with causing him to seek ways of escaping from belief in a merely mechanistic universe. His philosophy was very obscure, and there was much in it that I never succeeded in understanding. He had always had a leaning toward Kant, of whom I thought ill, and when he began to develop his own philosophy he was considerably influenced by Bergson. He was impressed by the aspect of unity in the universe, and considered that it is only through this aspect that scientific inferences can be justified. My temperament led me in the opposite direction, but I doubt whether pure reason could have decided which of us was more nearly in the right. Those who prefer his outlook might say that while he aimed at bringing comfort to plain people I aimed at bringing discomfort to philosophers; one who favored my outlook might retort that while he pleased the philosophers, I amused the plain people. However that may be, we went our separate ways, though affection survived to the last.

Whitehead was a man of extraordinarily wide interests, and his knowledge of history used to amaze me. At one time I discovered by chance that he was using that very serious and rather out-of-the-way work, Paolo Sarpi's *History of the Council of Trent*, as a bed book. Whatever historical subjects came up he could always supply some illuminating fact, such, for example, as the connection of Burke's political opinions with his interests in the City, and the relation of the Hussite heresy to the Bohemian silver mines. No one ever mentioned this to me again until a few years ago, when I was sent a learned monograph on the subject. I had no idea where Whitehead had got his information. But I have lately learned from Mr. John Kennair Peel that Whitehead's information probably came from Count Lützow's *Bohemia: an historical sketch*. Whitehead had delightful humor and great gentleness. When I was an undergraduate he was given the nickname of "the Cherub," which those who knew him in later life would think unduly disrespectful, but which at the time suited him. His family came from Kent and had been clergymen ever since about the time of the landing of St. Augustine in that county. In a book by Lucien Price recording his dialogues in America, Whitehead describes the prevalence of smuggling in the Isle of Thanet at the beginning of the nineteenth century when brandy and wine used to be hidden in the vaults of the church with the approbation of the vicar: "And more than once," he remarked, "when word was brought during service that officers were coming up the road, the whole congregation adjourned to get that liquor out of the way—assisted by the vicar. That is evidence of how intimately the Established Church shares the life of the nation." The Isle of Thanet dominated the Whitehead that I knew. His grandfather had migrated to it from the Isle of Sheppey and, according to Whitehead, was said by his friends to have composed a hymn containing the following sublime stanza:

> Lord of the Lambkin and the Lion,
> Lord of Jerusalem and Mount Zion,
> Lord of the Comet and the Planet,
> Lord of Sheppey and the Isle of Thanet!

I am glad that my first meeting with him was in the Isle of Thanet, for that region had a much more intimate place in his makeup than Cambridge ever had. I felt that Lucien Price's book ought to be called *Whitehead in Partibus*, "Partibus" being not everything outside England, but everything outside the Isle of Thanet.

He used to relate with amusement that my grandfather, who was much exercised by the spread of Roman Catholicism, adjured Whitehead's sister never to desert the Church of England. What amused him was that the contingency was so very improbable. Whitehead's theological opinions were not orthodox, but something of the vicarage atmosphere remained in his ways of feeling and came out in his later philosophical writings.

He was a very modest man, and his most extreme boast was that he did try to have the qualities of his defects. He never minded telling stories against himself. There were two old ladies in Cambridge who were sisters and whose manners suggested that they came straight out of *Cranford*. They were, in fact, advanced and even daring in their opinions, and were in the forefront of every movement of reform. White-head used to relate somewhat ruefully, how when he first met them he was misled by their exterior and thought it would be fun to shock them a little. But when he advanced some slightly radical opinion they said, "Oh, Mr. Whitehead, we are so pleased to hear *you* say that," showing that they had hitherto viewed him as a pillar of reaction.

His capacity for concentration on work was quite extraordinary. One hot summer's day, when I was staying with him at Grantchester, our friend Crompton Davies arrived and I took him into the garden to say how-do-you-do to his host. Whitehead was sitting writing mathematics. Davies and I stood in front of him at a distance of no more than a yard and watched him covering page after page with symbols. He never saw us, and after a time we went away with a feeling of awe.

Those who knew Whitehead well became aware of many things in him which did not appear in more casual contacts. Socially he appeared kindly, rational, and imperturbable, but he was not in fact imperturbable, and was certainly not that inhuman monster "the rational man." His devotion to his wife and his children was profound and passionate. He was at all times deeply aware of the importance of religion. As a young man, he was all but converted to Roman Catholicism by the influence of Cardinal Newman. His later philosophy gave him some part of what he wanted from religion. Like other men who lead extremely disciplined lives, he was liable to distressing soliloquies, and when he thought he was alone he would mutter abuse of himself for his supposed shortcomings. The early years of his marriage were much clouded by financial anxieties, but, although he found this very difficult to bear, he never let it turn him aside from work that was important but not lucrative.

He had practical abilities which at the time when I knew him best did not find very much scope. He had a kind of shrewdness which was surprising and which enabled him to get his way on committees in a manner astonishing to those who thought of him as wholly abstract and unworldly. He might have been an able administrator but for one defect, which was a complete inability to answer letters. I once wrote a letter to him on a mathematical point, as to which I urgently needed an answer for an article I was writing against Poincaré. He did not answer, so I wrote again. He still did not answer, so I telegraphed. As he was still silent, I sent a reply-paid telegram. But in the end, I had to travel down to Broadstairs to get the answer. His friends gradually got to know this peculiarity, and on the rare occasions when any of them got a letter from him they would all assemble to congratulate the recipient. He justified himself by saying that if he answered letters, he would have no time for original work. I think the justification was complete and unanswerable.

Whitehead was extraordinarily perfect as a teacher. He took a personal interest in those with whom he had to deal and knew both their strong and their weak points. He would elicit from a pupil the best of which a pupil was capable. He was never repressive, or sarcastic, or superior, or any of the things that inferior teachers like to be. I think that in all the abler young men with whom he came in contact he inspired, as he did in me, a very real and lasting affection.

Sidney and Beatrice Webb

SIDNEY and Beatrice Webb, whom I knew intimately for a number of years, at times even sharing a house with them, were the most completely married couple that I have ever known. They were, however, very averse from any romantic view of love or marriage. Marriage was a social institution designed to fit instinct into a legal framework. During the first ten years of their marriage, Mrs. Webb would remark at intervals, "as Sidney always says, marriage is the wastepaper basket of the emotions." In later years there was a slight change. They would generally have a couple to stay with them for the weekend, and on Sunday afternoon they would go for a brisk walk, Sidney with the lady and Beatrice with the gentleman. At a certain point, Sidney would remark, "I know just what Beatrice is saying at this moment. She is saying, 'as Sidney always says, marriage is the wastepaper basket of the emotions.'" Whether Sidney ever really did say this is not known.

I knew Sidney before his marriage. But he was then much less than half of what the two of them afterward became. Their collaboration was quite dovetailed. I used to think, though this was perhaps an undue simplification, that she had the ideas and he did the work. He was perhaps the most industrious man that I have ever known. When they were writing a book on local government, they would send circulars to all local government officials throughout the country asking questions and pointing out that the official in question could legally purchase their forthcoming book out of the rates. When I let my house to them, the postman, who was an ardent Socialist, did not know whether to be more honored by serving them or annoyed at having to deliver a thousand answers a day to their circulars. Webb was originally a second division clerk in the Civil Service, but by immense industry succeeded in rising into the first division. He was somewhat earnest, and did not like jokes on sacred subjects such as political theory. On one occasion I remarked to him that democracy has at least one merit, namely, that a member of Parliament cannot be stupider than his constituents, for the more stupid he is, the more stupid they were to elect him. Webb was seriously annoyed and said bitingly, "That is the sort of argument I don't like."

Mrs. Webb had a wider range of interests than her husband. She took considerable interest in individual human beings, not only when they could be useful. She was deeply religious without belonging to any recognized brand of orthodoxy, though as a Socialist she preferred the Church of England because it was a State institution. She was one of nine sisters, the daughters of a self-made man named Potter who acquired most of his fortune by building huts for the armies in the Crimea. He was a disciple of Herbert Spencer, and Mrs. Webb was the most notable product of that philosopher's theories of education. I am sorry to say that my mother, who was her neighbor in the country, described her as a "social butterfly," but one may hope that she would have modified this judgment if she had known Mrs. Webb in later life. When she became interested in socialism she decided to sample the Fabians, especially the three most distinguished, who were Webb, Shaw, and Graham Wallas. There was something like the Judgment of Paris with the sexes reversed, and it was Sidney who emerged as the counterpart of Aphrodite.

Webb had been entirely dependent upon his earnings, whereas Beatrice had inherited a competence from her father. Beatrice had the mentality of the governing class, which Sidney had not. Seeing that they had enough to live on without earning, they decided to devote their lives to research and to the higher branches of propaganda. In both they were amazingly successful. Their books are a tribute to their industry, and the School of Economics is a tribute to Sidney's skill. I do not think that Sidney's abilities would have been nearly as fruitful as they were if they had not been backed by Beatrice's self-confidence. I asked her once whether in her youth she had ever had any feeling of shyness. "Oh no," she said, "if I ever felt inclined to be timid as I was going into a room full of people, I would say to myself, 'You're the cleverest member of one of the cleverest families in the cleverest class of the cleverest nation in the world, why should you be frightened?' "

I both liked and admired Mrs. Webb, although I disagreed with her about many very important matters. I admired first and foremost her ability, which was very great. I admired next her integrity: she lived for public objects and was never deflected by personal ambition, although she was not devoid of it. I liked her because she was a warm and kind friend to those for whom she had a personal affection, but I disagreed with her about religion, about imperialism, and about the worship of the State. This last was of the essence of Fabianism. It had led both the Webbs and also Shaw into what I thought an undue tolerance of Mussolini and Hitler, and ultimately into a rather absurd adulation of the Soviet government.

But nobody is all of a piece, not even the Webbs. I once remarked to Shaw that Webb seemed to me somewhat deficient in kindly feeling. "No," Shaw replied, "you are quite mistaken. Webb and I were once in a tram car in Holland eating biscuits out of a bag. A handcuffed criminal was brought into the tram by policemen. All the other passengers shrank away in horror, but Webb went up to the prisoner and offered him biscuits." I remember this story whenever I find myself becoming unduly critical of either Webb or Shaw.

There were people whom the Webbs hated. They hated Wells, both because he offended Mrs. Webb's rigid Victorian morality and because he tried to dethrone Webb from his reign over the Fabian Society. They hated Ramsay MacDonald from very early days. The least hostile thing that I ever heard either of them say about him was at the time of the formation of the first Labor Government, when Mrs. Webb said he was a very good substitute for a leader.

Their political history was rather curious. At first they operated with the Conservatives because Mrs. Webb was pleased with Arthur Balfour for being willing to give more public money to Church Schools. When the Conservatives fell in 1906, the Webbs made some slight and ineffectual efforts to collaborate with the Liberals. But at last it occurred to them that as Socialists they might feel more at home in the Labor Party, of which in their later years they were loyal members.

For a number of years Mrs. Webb was addicted to fasting, from motives partly hygienic and partly religious. She would have no breakfast and a very meager dinner. Her only solid meal was lunch. She almost always had a number of distinguished people to lunch, but she would get so hungry that the moment it was announced she marched in ahead of all her guests and started to eat. She nevertheless believed that starvation made her more spiritual, and once told me that it gave her exquisite visions. "Yes," I replied, "if you eat too little, you see visions; and if you drink too much, you see snakes." I am afraid she thought this remark inexcusably flippant. Webb did not share the religious side of her nature, but was in no degree hostile to it, in spite of the fact that it was sometimes inconvenient to him. When they and I were staying at a hotel in Normandy, she used to stay upstairs since she could not bear the painful spectacle of us breakfasting. Sidney, however, would come down for rolls and coffee. The first morning Mrs. Webb sent a message by the maid, "we do not have butter for Sidney's breakfast." Her use of "we" was one of the delights of their friends.

Both of them were fundamentally undemocratic, and regarded it as the function of a statesman to bamboozle or terrorize the populace. I realized the origins of Mrs. Webb's conceptions of government when she repeated to me her father's description of shareholders' meetings. It is the recognized function of directors to keep shareholders in their place, and she had a similar view about the relation of the government to the electorate.

Her father's stories of his career had not given her any undue respect for the great. After he had built huts for the winter quarters of the French armies in the Crimea, he went to Paris to get paid. He had spent almost all his capital in putting up the huts, and payment became important to him. But, although everybody in Paris admitted the debt, the check did not come. At last he met Lord Brassey who had come on a similar errand. When Mr. Potter explained his difficulties, Lord Brassey laughed at him and said, "My dear fellow, you don't know the ropes. You must give fifty pounds to the

Minister and five pounds to each of his underlings." Mr. Potter did so, and the check came next day.

Sidney had no hesitation in using wiles which some would think unscrupulous. He told me, for example, that when he wished to carry some point through a committee where the majority thought otherwise, he would draw up a resolution in which the contentious point occurred twice. He would have a long debate about its first occurrence and at last give way graciously. Nine times out of ten, so he concluded, no one would notice that the same point occurred later in the same resolution.

The Webbs did a great work in giving intellectual backbone to British Socialism. They performed more or less the same function that the Benthamites at an earlier time had performed for the Radicals. The Webbs and the Benthamites shared a certain dryness and a certain coldness and a belief that the wastepaper basket is the place for the emotions. But the Benthamites and the Webbs alike taught their doctrines to enthusiasts. Bentham and Robert Owen could produce a well-balanced intellectual progeny and so could the Webbs and Keir Hardy. One should not demand of anybody all the things that add value to a human being. To have some of them is as much as should be demanded. The Webbs pass this test, and indubitably the British Labor Party would have been much more wild and woolly if they had never existed. Their mantle descended upon Mrs. Webb's nephew Sir Stafford Cripps, and but for them I doubt whether the British democracy would have endured with the same patience the arduous years through which we have been passing.

D. H. Lawrence

M Y ACQUAINTANCE with Lawrence was brief and hectic, lasting altogether about a year. We were brought together by Lady Ottoline Morrell who admired us both and made us think that we ought to admire each other. Pacifism had produced in me a mood of bitter rebellion and I found Lawrence equally full of rebellion. This made us think, at first, that there was a considerable measure of agreement between us, and it was only gradually that we discovered that we differed from each other more than either differed from the Kaiser.

There were in Lawrence at that time two attitudes to the war: on the one hand, he could not be wholeheartedly patriotic, because his wife was German; but on the other hand, he had such a hatred of mankind that he tended to think both sides must be right in so far as they hated each other. As I came to know these attitudes, I realized that neither was one with which I could sympathize. Awareness of our differences, however, was gradual on both sides and at first all went merry as a marriage bell. I invited him to visit me at Cambridge and introduced him to Keynes and a number of other people. He hated them all with a passionate hatred and said they were "dead, dead, dead." For a time I thought he might be right. I liked Lawrence's fire, I liked the energy and passion of his feelings, I liked his belief that something very fundamental was needed to put the world right. I agreed with him in thinking that politics could not be divorced from individual psychology. I felt him to be a man of a certain imaginative genius and, at first, when I felt inclined to disagree with him, I thought that perhaps his insight into human nature was deeper than mine. It was only gradually that I came to feel him a positive force for evil and that he came to have the same feeling about me.

I was at this time preparing a course of lectures which was afterward published as *Principles of Social Reconstruction.* He also wanted to lecture, and for the time it seemed possible that there might be some sort of loose collaboration between us. We exchanged a number of letters of which mine are lost but his have been published. In his letters the gradual awareness of the consciousness of our fundamental disagreements can be traced. I was a firm believer in democracy, whereas he had developed the whole philosophy of fascism before the politicians had thought of it. "I don't believe," he wrote, "in democratic control. I think the working man is fit to elect governors or overseers for his immediate circumstances, but for no more. You must utterly revise the electorate. The working man shall elect superiors for the things that concern him immediately, no more. From the other classes, as they rise, shall be elected the higher governors. The thing must culminate in one real head, as every organic thing must—no foolish republics with foolish presidents, but an elected king, something like Julius Caesar." He, of course, in his imagination, supposed that when a dictatorship was established he would be the Julius Caesar. This was part of the dreamlike quality of all his thinking. He never let himself bump into reality. He would go into long tirades about how one must proclaim "the Truth" to the multitude, and he seemed to have no doubt that the multitude would listen. I asked him what method he was going to adopt. Would he put his political philosophy into a book? No: in our corrupt society the written word is always a lie. Would he go into Hyde Park and proclaim "the Truth" from a soap box? No: that would be far too dangerous (odd streaks of prudence emerged in him from time to time). Well, I said, what would you do? At this point he would change the subject.

Gradually I discovered that he had no real wish to make the world better, but only to indulge in eloquent soliloquy about how bad it was. If anybody overheard the soliloquies so much the better, but they were designed at most to produce a little faithful band of disciples who could sit in the deserts of New Mexico and feel holy. All this was conveyed to me in the language of a fascist dictator as what I *must* preach, the "must" having thirteen underlinings.

His letters grew gradually more hostile. He wrote: "What's the good of living as you do anyway? I don't believe your lectures *are* good. They are nearly over, aren't they? What's the good of sticking in the damned ship and haranguing the merchant pilgrims in their own language? Why don't you drop overboard? Why don't you clear out of the whole show? One must be an outlaw these days, not a teacher or preacher." This seemed to me mere rhetoric. I was becoming more of an outlaw than he ever was and I could not quite see his ground of complaint against me. He phrased his complaint in different ways at different times. On another occasion he wrote: "Do stop working and writing altogether and become a creature instead of a mechanical instrument. Do clear out of the whole social ship. Do for your very pride's sake become a mere nothing, a mole, a creature that feels its way and doesn't think. Do for heaven's sake be a baby, and not a savant any more. Don't *do* anything more—but for heaven's sake begin to *be*. Start at the very beginning and be a perfect baby: in the name of courage.

"Oh, and I want to ask you, when you make your will, do leave me enough to live on. I want you to live forever. But I want you to make me in some part your heir." The only difficulty with this program was that if I adopted it I should have nothing to leave.

He had a mystical philosophy of "blood" which I disliked. "There is," he said, "another seat of consciousness than the brain—and nerves. There is a blood consciousness which exists in us independently of the ordinary mental consciousness. One lives, knows and has one's being in the blood, without any reference to nerves and brain. This is one half of life belonging to the darkness. When I take a woman, then the blood percept is supreme. My blood knowing is overwhelming. We should realize that we have a blood being, a blood consciousness, a blood soul complete and apart from a mental and nerve consciousness." This seemed to me frankly rubbish, and I rejected it vehemently, though I did not then know that it led straight to Auschwitz.

He always got into a fury if one suggested that anybody could possibly have kindly feelings toward anybody else, and when I objected to war because of the suffering that it causes, he accused me of hypocrisy. "It isn't in the least true that you, your basic self, want ultimate peace. You are satisfying in an indirect, false way your lust to jab and strike. Either satisfy it in a direct and honorable way, saying 'I hate you all, liars and swine, and I am out to set upon you,' or stick to mathematics, where you can be true. But to come as the angel of peace—no, I prefer Tirpitz a thousand times in that role."

I find it difficult now to understand the devastating effect that this letter had upon me. I was inclined to believe that he had some insight denied to me, and when he said that my pacifism was rooted in blood lust I supposed he must be right. For twenty-four hours I thought that I was not fit to live and contemplated committing suicide. But at the end of that time, a healthier reaction set in, and I decided to have done with such morbidness. When he said that I *must* preach his doctrines and not mine I rebelled and told him to remember that he was no longer a schoolmaster and I was not his pupil. He had written, "The enemy of all mankind you are, full of the lust of enmity. It is *not* a hatred of falsehood which inspires you, it is the hatred of people of flesh and blood, it is a perverted mental blood lust. Why don't you own it? Let us become strangers again. I think it is better." I thought so too. But he found a pleasure in denouncing me and continued for some months to write letters containing sufficient friendliness to keep the correspondence alive. In the end, it faded away without any dramatic termination.

What at first attracted me to Lawrence was a certain dynamic quality and a habit of challenging assumptions that one is apt to take for granted. I was already accustomed to being accused of undue slavery to reason and I thought perhaps that he could give me a vivifying dose of unreason. I did in fact acquire a certain stimulus from him, and I think the book that I wrote in spite of his blasts of denunciation was better than it would have been if I had not known him.

But this is not to say that there was anything good in his ideas. I do not think in retrospect that they had any merit whatever. They were the ideas of a sensitive would-be despot who got angry with the world because it would not instantly obey. When he realized that other people existed, he hated them. But most of the time he lived in a solitary world of his own imaginings, peopled by phantoms as fierce as he wished them to be. His excessive emphasis on sex was due to the fact that in sex alone he was compelled to admit that he was not the only human being in the universe. But it was because this admission was so painful that he conceived of sex relations as a perpetual fight in which each is attempting to destroy the other.

The world between the wars was attracted to madness. Of this attraction Nazism was the most emphatic expression. Lawrence was a suitable exponent of this cult of insanity. I am not sure whether the cold inhuman sanity of Stalin was any improvement.

Lord John Russell

M Y GRANDFATHER, whom I remember vividly, was
born on the eighteenth of August, 1792, a fort-
night after the poet Shelley, whose life ended in
1822. At the moment of my grandfather's birth the French
Revolution was just getting under way, and it was in the
month of his birth that the monarchy fell. He was one month
old when the September Massacres terrified Royalists at
home and the Battle of Valmy began the twenty-two years'
war of the revolution against reaction. In this war, my grandfather, as became a follower of Fox, was more or less what
would now be called a "fellow traveler." His first (unpublished) work contained an ironical dedication to Pitt, then still
Prime Minister. During the Peninsular War he traveled in
Spain, but with no wish to fight against Napoleon. He visited
Napoleon in Elba, and had his ear pulled by the Great Man
as was usual. When Napoleon returned from Elba my grandfather, who had been for two years a Member of Parliament,
made a speech urging that he should not be opposed. The
Government, however, being in the hands of the Tories, decided otherwise, and the Battle of Waterloo was the result.
His greatest achievement was the carrying of the Reform Bill
in 1832, which started Britain on the course that led to complete democracy. The opposition to this Bill on the part of
the Tories was very violent and almost led to civil war. The
clash at this time was the decisive battle between reactionaries and progressives in England. It was the peaceful victory
in this battle that saved England from revolution, and it was

my grandfather who did most to secure the victory. He had after this a long career in politics and was twice Prime Minister, but did not again have the opportunity to lead decisively at a great crisis. In his later years he was only moderately liberal, except in one respect, and that was his hatred of religious disabilities. When he was a young man all who were not members of the Church of England suffered grave political disabilities. Jews especially were excluded from both Houses of Parliament and from many offices by means of an oath which only Christians could take. I still remember vividly seeing a large gathering of earnest men on the lawn in front of our house on May 9, 1878, when he was within a few days of his death. They cheered, and I naturally inquired what they were cheering about. I was told that they were leading nonconformists congratulating him on the fiftieth anniversary of his first great achievement, the repeal of the Test and Corporation Acts, which excluded nonconformists from office and Parliament. The love of civil and religious liberty was very firmly implanted in me by such incidents and by the teaching of history that illuminated them. This feeling has survived through the various totalitarian regimes that have seduced many of my friends of the Right and of the Left equally.

As my parents were dead, I lived in my grandfather's house during the last two years of his life. Even at the beginning of this time his physical powers were much impaired. I remember him out of doors being wheeled in a Bath chair, and I remember him sitting reading in his sitting room. My recollection, which is of course unreliable, is that he was always reading Parliamentary Reports of which bound volumes covered all the walls of the large hall. At the time to which this recollection refers, he was contemplating action connected with the Russo-Turkish War of 1876, but ill health made that impossible.

In public life he was often accused of coldness, but at home he was warm and affectionate and kindly in the highest degree. He liked children, and I do not remember any single occasion when he told me not to make a noise or said any of the other repressive things that old people are apt to say to the very young. He was a good linguist and had no difficulty in making speeches in French or Spanish or Italian. He used to sit shaking with laughter over *Don Quixote* in the original. Like all Liberals of his time he had a romantic love of Italy, and the Italian Government gave him a large statue representing Italy, to express their gratitude for his services in the cause of Italian unity. This statue always stood in his sitting room and greatly interested me.

My grandfather belonged to a type which is now quite extinct, the type of the aristocratic reformer whose zeal is derived from the classics, from Demosthenes and Tacitus, rather than from any more recent source. They worshiped a goddess called Liberty, but her lineaments were rather vague. There was also a demon called Tyranny. He was rather more definite. He was represented by kings and priests and policemen, especially if they were aliens. This creed had inspired the intellectual revolutionaries of France, though Madame Roland on the scaffold found it somewhat too simple. It was this creed that inspired Byron, and led him to fight for Greece. It was this creed that inspired Mazzini and Garibaldi and their English admirers. As a creed it was literary and poetic and romantic. It was quite untouched by the hard facts of economics which dominate all modern political thinking. My grandfather, as a boy, had as tutor Dr. Cartwright, the inventor of the power loom, which was one

of the main factors in the Industrial Revolution. My grandfather never knew that he had made this invention, but admired him for his elegant Latinity and for the elevation of
his moral sentiments, as well as for the fact that he was the
brother of a famous radical agitator.

My grandfather subscribed to democracy as an ideal, but
was by no means anxious that the approach to it should be
in any way precipitate. He favored a gradual extension of
the franchise, but I think he was convinced that, however it
might be extended, English reforming parties would always
find their leaders in the great Whig families. I do not mean
that he was consciously convinced of this, but that it was
part of the air he breathed, something which could be taken
for granted without discussion.

Pembroke Lodge, where my grandfather lived, was a
house in the middle of Richmond Park about ten miles from
the center of London. It was in the gift of the Queen, and
was given by her to my grandfather for his lifetime and that
of my grandmother. In this house many Cabinet meetings
took place and to this house many famous men came. On one
occasion the Shah of Persia came and my grandfather apolo-
gized for the smallness of the house. The Shah replied po-
litely, "Yes, it is a small house, but it contains a great man."
In this house I met Queen Victoria when I was two years
old. I was much interested by the visit of three Chinese diplomats in the correct Chinese ceremonial costume of that
day; also by the visit of two Negro emissaries from Liberia.
There was in the drawing room an exquisite inlaid Japanese
table given to my grandfather by the Japanese Government.
On sideboards in the dining room there were two enormous
porcelain vases, which were presents from the King of
Saxony. There was a narrow space between a table and a
china cabinet which I was strictly forbidden to squeeze

through, and, on this ground, it was always called the Dardanelles. Every corner of the house was associated with some nineteenth-century event or institution which now seems as remotely historical as the dodo. Everything belonging to my childhood was part of a now completely vanished world—the rambling Victorian house, now no longer in the gift of the sovereign, but turned into a tea shop; the garden, formerly full of nooks and crannies in which a child could hide, but now wide open to the general public; the courtly diplomats representing sovereigns of States now vanished or turned into republics; the solemn pompous men of letters, to whom every platitude seemed profound; and above all, the absolute conviction of stability which made it an unquestioned axiom that no changes were to be expected anywhere in the world, except an ordered and gradual development toward a constitution exactly like that of Britain. Was ever an age so blessedly blind to the future? Cassandra truly prophesied disaster and was not believed; the men of my grandfather's age falsely prophesied prosperity and were believed. If he could come back into our present world he would be far more bewildered than *his* grandfather would have been by the nineteenth century. For those who have grown up in the atmosphere of a strong tradition, adaptation to the world of the present is difficult. Awareness of this difficulty makes it possible to understand how in the past and in the present great empires and great institutions, which have stood for ages, can be swept away because the political experience that they embody has suddenly become useless and inapplicable. For this reason our age produces bewilderment in many, but offers at the same time a possibly fruitful challenge to those who are capable of new thought and new imagination.

John Stuart Mill

I T IS not easy to assess the importance of John Stuart Mill in nineteenth-century England. What he achieved depended more upon his moral elevation and his just estimate of the ends of life than upon any purely intellectual merits.

His influence in politics and in forming opinion on moral issues was very great and, to my mind, wholly good. Like other eminent Victorians he combined intellectual distinction with a very admirable character. This intellectual distinction gave weight to his opinions, and was thought at the time to be greater than it appears in retrospect. There are various modern trends which are adverse also to his ethical and moral theories, but in these respects I cannot feel that the world has made any advance since his day.

Intellectually, he was unfortunate in the date of his birth. His predecessors were pioneers in one direction and his successors in another. The substructure of his opinions remained always that which had been laid down for him in youth by the dominating personality of his father, but the theories which he built upon this substructure were very largely such as it could not support. Skyscrapers, I am told, cannot be built in London because they need to be founded on rock. Mill's doctrines, like a skyscraper founded on clay, were shaky because the foundations were continually sinking. The new stories, which he added under the inspiration of Carlyle and Mrs. Taylor, were intellectually insecure. To put the matter in another way: morals and intellect were perpetually at war in his thought, morals being incarnate in Mrs. Taylor and intellect in his father. If the one was too soft, the other was too harsh. The amalgam which resulted was practically beneficent, but theoretically somewhat incoherent.

Mill's first important book was his *Logic*, which no doubt presented itself in his mind as a plea for experimental rather than a priori methods, and, as such, it was useful though not very original. He could not foresee the immense and surprising development of deductive logic which began with Boole's *Laws of Thought* in 1854, but only proved its importance at a considerably later date. Everything that Mill has to say in his *Logic* about matters other than inductive inference is perfunctory and conventional. He states, for example, that propositions are formed by putting together two names, one of which is the subject and the other the predicate. This, I am sure, appeared to him an innocuous truism; but it had been, in fact, the source of two thousand years of important error. On the subject of names, with which modern logic has been much concerned, what he has to say is totally inadequate, and is, in fact, not so good as what had been said by Duns Scotus and William of Occam. His famous contention that the syllogism in Barbara is a *petitio principii*, and that the argument is really from particulars to particulars, has a measure of truth in certain cases, but cannot be accepted as a general doctrine. He maintains, for example, that the proposition "all men are mortal" asserts "the Duke of Wellington is mortal" even if the person making the assertion has never heard of the Duke of Wellington. This is obviously untenable: a person who knows the meaning of the words "man" and "mortal" can understand the statement "all men are mortal" but can make no inference about a man he has never heard of; whereas, if Mill were right about the Duke of Wellington, a man could not understand this statement unless he knew the catalogue of all the men who ever have existed or ever will exist. His doctrine that inference is from particulars to particulars is correct psychology when applied to what I call "animal induction," but is never correct logic. To infer, from the mortality of men in the past, the mortality of those not yet dead, can only be legitimate if there is a *general* principle of induction. Broadly speaking, no general conclusion can be drawn without a general premise, and only a general premise will warrant a general conclusion from an incomplete enumeration of instances. What is more, there are general propositions of which no one can doubt the truth, although not a single instance of them can be given. Take, for example, the following: "All the whole numbers which no one will have thought of before the year A.D. 2000, are greater than a million." You cannot attempt to give me an instance without contradicting yourself, and you cannot pretend that all the whole numbers have been thought of by someone. From the time of Locke onward, British empiricists had had theories of knowledge which were inapplicable to mathematics; while Continental philosophers, with the exception of the French *Philosophes*, by an undue emphasis upon mathematics, had produced fantastic metaphysical systems. It was only after Mill's time that the sphere of empiricism was clearly delimited from that of mathematics and logic so that peaceful co-existence became possible. I first read Mill's *Logic* at the age of eighteen, and at that time I had a very strong bias in his favor; but even then I could not believe that our acceptance of the proposition "two and two are four" was a generalization from experience. I was quite at a loss to say how we arrived at this knowledge, but it *felt* quite different from such a proposition as "all swans are white," which experience might, and in fact did, confute. It did not seem to me that a fresh instance of two and two being four in any degree strengthened my belief. But it is only the modern development of mathematical logic which has enabled me to justify these early feelings and to fit mathematics and empirical knowledge into a single framework.

Mill, although he knew a certain amount of mathematics, never learned to think in a mathematical way. His law of causation is not one which is employed in mathematical physics. It is a practical maxim employed by savages and philosophers in the conduct of daily life, but not employed in physics by anyone acquainted with the calculus. The laws of physics never state, as Mill's causal laws do, that A is always followed by B. They assert only that when A is present, there will be certain directions of change; since A also changes, the directions of change are themselves continually changing. The notion that causal laws are of the form "A causes B" is altogether too atomic, and could never have been entertained by anybody who had imaginatively apprehended the continuity of change.

But let us not be too dogmatic. There are those who say that physical changes are not continuous but explosive. These people, however, also say that individual events are not subject to any causal regularity, and that the apparent regularities of the world are only due to the law of averages. I do not know whether this doctrine is right or wrong; but, in any case, it is very different from Mill's.

Mill's law of causation is, in fact, only roughly and approximately true in an everyday and unscientific sense. Nevertheless, he thinks it is proved by an inference which elsewhere he considers very shaky: that of induction by simple enumeration. This process is not only shaky, but can be proved quite definitely to lead to false consequences more often than to true ones. If you find n objects all of which possess two properties, A and B, and you then find another object possessing the property A, it can easily be proved that it is unlikely to possess the property B. This is concealed from common sense by the fact that our animal propensity toward induction is confined to the sort of cases in which induction is liable to give correct results. Take the following as an example of an induction which no one would make: all the sheep that Kant ever saw were within ten miles of Königsberg, but he felt no inclination to induce that all sheep were within ten miles of Königsberg.

Modern physics does not use induction in the old sense at all. It makes enormous theories without pretending that they are in any exact sense true, and uses them only hypothetically until new facts turn up which require new theories. All that the modern physicist claims for a theory is that it fits the known facts and therefore cannot at present be refuted. The problem of induction in its traditional form has by most theoretical physicists been abandoned as insoluble. I am not by any means persuaded that they are right in this, but I think it is quite definitely demonstrable that the problem is very different from what Mill supposed it to be.

It is rather surprising that Mill was so little influenced by Darwin and the theory of evolution. This is the more curious as he frequently quotes Herbert Spencer. He seems to have accepted the Darwinian theory but without realizing its implications. In the chapter on "Classification" in his Logic, he speaks of "natural kinds" in an entirely pre-Darwinian fashion, and even suggests that the recognized species of animals and plants are infimae species in the scholastic sense, although Darwin's book on the Origin of Species proved this view to be untenable. It was natural that the first edition of his Logic, which appeared in 1843, should take no account of the theory of evolution, but it is odd that no modifications were made in later editions. What is perhaps still more surprising is that in his *Three Essays on Religion*, written very late in his life, he does not reject the argument from design based upon the adaptation of plants and animals to their environment, or discuss Darwin's explanation of this adaptation. I do not think that he ever imaginatively conceived of man as one among animals or escaped from the eighteenth-century belief that man is fundamentally rational. I am thinking, now, not of what he would have explicitly professed, but of what he unconsciously supposed whenever he was not on his guard. Most of us go about the world with such subconscious presuppositions which influence our beliefs more than explicit arguments do, and in most of us these presuppositions are fully formed by the time we are twenty-five. In the case of Mill, Mrs. Taylor effected certain changes, but these were not in the purely intellectual realm. In that realm, James continued to reign supreme over his son's subconscious.

II

THE *Principles of Political Economy* was Mill's second major work. The first edition appeared in 1848, but it was followed by a substantially modified edition in the next year. Mr. Packe, in his admirable biography, has said most of what needs to be said about the difference between these two editions. The difference was mainly concerned with the question of Socialism. In the first edition, Socialism was criticized from the point of view of the orthodox tradition. But this shocked Mrs. Taylor, and she induced Mill to make very considerable modifications when a new edition was called for. One of the most valuable things in Mr. Packe's book is that he has at last enabled us to see Mrs. Taylor in an impartial light, and to understand the sources of her influence on Mill. But I think perhaps Mr. Packe is a little too severe in criticizing Mill for his change as regards Socialism. I cannot but think that what Mrs. Taylor did for him in this respect was to enable him to think what his own nature led him to think, as opposed to what he had been taught. His attitude to Socialism, as it appears in the later editions of the book, is by no means uncritical. He still feels that there are difficulties which Socialists do not adequately face. He says, for example, "It is the common error of Socialists to overlook the natural indolence of mankind"; and on this ground he fears that a Socialist community might stagnate. He lived in a happier age than ours: we should feel a joyful ecstasy if we could hope for anything as comfortable as stagnation.

In his chapter on "The Probable Futurity of the Laboring Classes" he develops a Utopia to which he looks forward. He hopes to see production in the hands of voluntary societies of workers. Production is not to be in the hands of the State, as Marxian Socialists have maintained that it should be. The Socialism to which Mill looks forward is that of St. Simon and Fourier. (Robert Owen, to my mind, is not sufficiently emphasized.) Pre-Marxian Socialism, which is that of which Mill writes, did not aim at increasing the power of the State. Mill argues emphatically that even under Socialism there will still have to be competition, though the competition will be between rival societies of workers, not between rival capitalists. He is inclined to admit that in such a Socialist system as he advocates the total production of goods might be less than under capitalism, but he contends that this would be no great evil provided everybody could be kept in reasonable comfort.

To readers of our time, who take it as part of the meaning of Socialism that private capitalists should be replaced by the

State, it is difficult to avoid misunderstanding in reading Mill. Mill preserved all the distrust of the State which the Manchester School had developed in fighting the feudal aristocracy; and the distrust which he derived from this source was strengthened by his passionate belief in liberty. The power of governments, he says, is always dangerous. He is confident that this power will diminish. Future ages, he maintains, will be unable to credit the amount of government interference which has hitherto existed. It is painful to read a statement of this sort, since it makes one realize the impossibility of foreseeing, even in its most general outlines, the course of future development. The only nineteenth-century writer who foresaw the future with any approach to accuracy was Nietzsche, and he foresaw it, not because he was wiser than other men, but because all the hateful things that have been happening were such as he wished to see. It is only in our disillusioned age that prophets like Orwell have begun to foretell what they feared rather than what they hoped.

Mill, both in his prophecies and in his hopes, was misled by not foreseeing the increasing power of great organizations. This applies not only in economics, but also in other spheres. He maintained, for example, that the State ought to insist upon universal education, but ought not to do the educating itself. He never realized that, so far as elementary education is concerned, the only important alternative to the State is the Church, which he would hardly have preferred.

Mill distinguishes between Communism and Socialism. He prefers the latter, while not wholly condemning the former. The distinction in his day was not so sharp as it has since become. Broadly speaking, as he explains it, the distinction is that Communists object to all private property while Socialists contend only that "land and the instruments of production should be the property, not of individuals, but of communities or associations, or of the Government." There is a famous passage in which he expresses his opinion on Communism:

"If, therefore, the choice were to be made between Communism with all its chances, and the present state of society with all its sufferings and injustices; if the institution of private property necessarily carried with it as a consequence, that the produce of labor should be apportioned as we now see it, almost in an inverse ratio to the labor—the largest portions to those who have never worked at all, the next largest to those whose work is almost nominal, and so in a descending scale, the remuneration dwindling as the work grows harder and more disagreeable, until the most fatiguing and exhausting bodily labor cannot count with certainty on being able to earn even the necessaries of life; if this or Communism were the alternative, all the difficulties, great or small, of Communism would be but as dust in the balance. But to make the comparison applicable, we must compare Communism at its best, with the regime of individual property, not as it is, but as it might be made. The principle of private property has never yet had a fair trial in any country; and less so, perhaps, in this country than in some others."

The history of words is curious. Nobody in Mill's time, with the possible exception of Marx, could have guessed that the word "Communism" would come to denote the military, administrative, and judicial tyranny of an oligarchy, permitting to the workers only so much of the produce of their labor as might be necessary to keep them from violent revolt. Marx, whom we can now see to have been the most influential of Mill's contemporaries, is, so far as I have been able to discover, not mentioned in any of Mill's writings, and it is quite probable that Mill never heard of him. *The Communist Manifesto* was published in the same year as Mill's *Political*

Economy, but the men who represented culture did not know of it. I wonder what unknown person in the present day will prove, a hundred years hence, to have been the dominant figure of our time.

Apart from the pronouncements on Socialism and Communism, Mill's *Political Economy* is not important. Its main principles are derived from his orthodox predecessors with only minor modifications. Ricardo's theory of value, with which on the whole he is in agreement, was superseded by Jevon's introduction of the concept of marginal utility, which represented an important theoretical improvement. As in his *Logic*, Mill is too ready to acquiesce in a traditional doctrine provided he is not aware of any practical evil resulting from it.

III

MUCH more important than Mill's longer treatises were his two short books *On the Subjection of Women* and *On Liberty*. In regard to the first of these, the world has gone completely as he would have wished. In regard to the second, there has been an exactly opposite movement.

It is a disgrace to both men and women that the world should have had to wait so long for champions of women's equality. Until the French Revolution, nobody except Plato ever thought of claiming equality for women, but when the subject came to be raised, incredibly ridiculous arguments were invented in support of the *status quo*. It was not only men who argued that women should have no part in politics. The arguments were equally convincing to women, and especially to political women such as Queen Victoria and Mrs.

Sidney Webb. Very few seemed capable of realizing that
the supremacy of men was based solely upon a supremacy
of muscle. The claim for women's equality was regarded as
a subject of ridicule, and remained so until three years before
it achieved success. I spoke in favor of votes for women before the First World War and in favor of pacifism during it.
The opposition which I encountered in the first of these
causes was more virulent and more widespread than that
which I encountered in the second. Few things in history
are more surprising than the sudden concession of political
rights to women in all civilized countries except Switzerland.
This is, I think, part of a general change from a biological to
a mechanistic outlook. Machinery diminishes the importance
of muscle. Industry is less concerned with the seasons than
agriculture. Democracy has destroyed dynasties and lessened
the feeling of family continuity. Napoleon wanted his son to
succeed him. Lenin, Stalin and Hitler had no such desire. I
think the concession of equality to women has been rendered
possible by the fact that they are no longer regarded primarily in a biological light. Mill remarks that the only women in
England who are not slaves and drudges are those who are
operatives in factories. Unaccountably, he forgot Queen Victoria. But there is a measure of truth in what he says, for the
work of women in factories, unlike childbearing, is such as
men are capable of doing. It seems that, however admirable
the emancipation of women may be in itself, it is part of a
vast sociological change emphasizing industry at the expense
of agriculture, the factory at the expense of the nursery, and
power at the expense of subsistence. I think the world has
swung too far in this direction and will not return to sanity
until the biological aspects of human life are again remembered. But I see no reason why, if this occurs, it should involve a revival of the subjection of women.

Mill's book *On Liberty* is more important to us in the present day than his book *On the Subjection of Women*. It is more important because the cause which it advocates has been less successful. There is, on the whole, much less liberty in the world now than there was a hundred years ago; and there is no reason to suppose that restrictions on liberty are likely to grow less in any foreseeable future. Mill points to Russia as a country so dominated by bureaucracy that no one, not even the individual bureaucrat, has any personal liberty. But the Russia of his day, after the emancipation of the serfs, had a thousand times more freedom than the Russia of our day. The Russia of his day produced great writers who opposed the autocracy, courageous revolutionaries who were able to carry on their propaganda in spite of prison and exile, even liberals among those in power, as the abolition of serfdom proved. There was every reason to hope that Russia would in time develop into a constitutional monarchy, marching by stages toward the degree of political freedom that existed in England. The growth of liberty was also apparent in other countries. In the United States, slavery was abolished a few years after the publication of Mill's book. In France, the monarchy of Napoleon III, which Mill passionately hated, came to an end eleven years after his book was published; and, at the same time, manhood suffrage was introduced in Germany. On such grounds I do not think that Mr. Packe is right in saying that the general movement of the time was against liberty, and I do not think that Mill's optimism was irrational.

With Mill's values, I for my part find myself in complete agreement. I think he is entirely right in emphasizing the importance of the individual in so far as values are concerned. I think, moreover, that it is even more desirable in our day than it was in his to uphold the kind of outlook for which he stands. But those who care for liberty in our day have to fight different battles from those of the nineteenth century, and have to devise new expedients if liberty is not to perish. From the seventeenth century to the end of the nineteenth, "Liberty" was the watchword of the radicals and revolutionaries; but in our day the word has been usurped by reactionaries, and those who think themselves most progressive are inclined to despise it. It is labeled as part of "rotten bourgeois idealism" and is regarded as a middle-class fad, important only to those who already enjoy the elegant leisure of the well-to-do. So far as any one person is responsible for this change, the blame must fall on Marx, who substituted Prussian discipline for freedom as both the means and the end of revolutionary action. But Marx would not have had the success which he has had if there had not been large changes in social organization and in technique which furthered his ideals as opposed to those of earlier reformers.

What has changed the situation since Mill's day is, as I remarked before, the great increase of organization. Every organization is a combination of individuals for a purpose; and, if this purpose is to be achieved, it requires a certain subordination of the individuals to the whole. If the purpose is one in which all the individuals feel a keen interest, and if the executive of the organization commands confidence, the sacrifice of liberty may be very small. But if the purpose for which the organization exists inspires only its executive, to which the other members submit for extraneous reasons, the loss of liberty involved may grow until it becomes almost total. The larger the organization, the greater becomes the gap in power between those at the top and those at the bottom, and the more likelihood there is of oppression. The modern world, for technical reasons, is very much more organized than the world of a hundred years ago: there are very many fewer acts which a man does simply from his own impulse, and very many more which he is compelled or induced to perform by some authority. The advantages that spring from organization are so great and so obvious that it would be absurd to wish to return to an earlier condition, but those who are conscious only of the advantages are apt to overlook the dangers, which are very real and very menacing.

As a first example, let us take agriculture. In the years immediately succeeding the publication of Mill's *Liberty*, there was an immense development of pioneering in the Middle West of the United States. The pioneers prided themselves upon their "rugged individualism." They settled in regions which were well wooded, well watered, and of great natural fertility. Without excessive labor, they felled the trees, thereby securing log cabins and fuel, and when the soil was cleared, they procured a rich harvest of grain. There was, however, a serpent in this individualist paradise: the serpent was the railroad, without which the grain could not be got to market. The railroad represented a vast accumulation of capital, an enormous expenditure of labor, and a combination of very many persons, hardly any of them agriculturists. The pioneers were indignant at their loss of independence, and their indignation gave rise to the Populist movement, which, in spite of much heat, never achieved any success. In this case, however, there was only one enemy of personal independence. I was struck by the difference when I came in contact with pioneers in Australia. The conquering of new land for agriculture in Australia depends upon enormously expensive schemes of irrigation, too vast for the separate states and only practicable by the federal government. Even then, when a man has acquired a tract of land, it contains no timber, and all his building materials and his fuel have to be brought from a distance. Medical attention for himself and his family is only rendered possible by an elaborate organization of airplanes and radio. His livelihood depends upon the export trade, which prospers or suffers according to the vagaries of distant governments. His mentality, his tastes and his feelings, are still those of the rugged individualist pioneer of a hundred years ago, but his circumstances are totally different. However he may wish to rebel, he is tightly controlled by forces that are entirely external to himself. Intellectual liberty he may still have; but economic liberty has become a dream.

But the life of the Australian pioneer is one of heavenly bliss when compared with that of the peasant in Communist countries, who has become more completely a serf than he was in the worst days of the Czardom. He owns no land, he has no right to the produce of his own labor, the authorities permit him only a bare subsistence, and any complaint may land him in a forced-labor camp. The totalitarian State is the last term of organization, the goal toward which, if we are not careful, we shall find all developed countries tending. Socialists have thought that the power hitherto vested in capitalists would become beneficent if vested in the State. To some degree this is true, so long as the State is democratic. Communists, unfortunately, forgot this proviso. By transferring economic power to an oligarchic State, they produced an engine of tyranny more dreadful, more vast, and at the same time more minute than any that had existed in previous history. I do not think this was the intention of those who made the Russian Revolution, but it was the effect of their actions. Their actions had this effect because they failed to realize the need of liberty and the inevitable evils of despotic power.

But the evils, of which the extreme form is seen in Communist countries, exist in a lesser degree, and may easily increase, in many countries belonging to what is somewhat humorously called the "Free World." Vavilov, the most distinguished geneticist that Russia has produced in recent times, was sent to perish miserably in the Arctic because he would not subscribe to Stalin's ignorant belief in the inheritance of acquired characters. Oppenheimer is disgraced and prevented from pursuing his work largely because he doubted the practicability of the hydrogen bomb at a time when this doubt was entirely rational. The FBI, which has only the level of education to be expected among policemen, considers itself competent to withhold visas from the most learned men in Europe on grounds which every person capable of understanding the matters at issue knows to be absurd. This evil has reached such a point that international conferences of learned men in the United States have become impossible. It is curious that Mill makes very little mention of the police as a danger to liberty. In our day, they are its worst enemy in most civilized countries.

IV

It is an interesting speculation, and perhaps not a wholly idle one, to consider how Mill would have written his book if he had been writing now. I think that everything he says on the *value* of liberty could stand unchanged. So long as human life persists, liberty will be essential to many of the greatest goods that our terrestrial existence has to offer. It has its profound source in one of our most elementary instincts: newborn infants fall into a rage if their limbs are constricted. The kinds of freedom that are desired change with growth in years and knowledge, but it remains an essential source of simple happiness. But it is not only happiness that is lost when liberty is needlessly impaired. It is also all the more important and difficult kinds of usefulness. Almost every great service that individuals have ever done to mankind has exposed them to violent hostility extending often to martyrdom. All this is said by Mill so well that it would require no alteration except the supplying of more recent instances.

Mill would, I think, go on to say that unwarrantable interferences with liberty are mostly derived from one or other of two sources: the first of these is a tyrannical moral code which demands of others conformity with rules of behavior which they do not accept; the other, which is the more important, is unjust power.

Of the first of these, the tyranny of moral codes, Mill gives various examples. He has an eloquent and powerful passage on the persecution of the Mormons, which is all the better for his purposes because no one could suspect him of thinking well of polygamy. Another of his examples of undue interference with liberty in the supposed interests of a moral code is the observance of the Sabbath, which has lost most of its importance since his day. My father, who was a disciple of Mill, spent his brief Parliamentary career in a vain endeavor to persuade the House of Commons that T. H. Huxley's lectures were not entertaining, for, if they could be considered as entertainment, they were illegal on Sundays.

I think if Mill were writing now he would choose in further illustration two matters which the police have recently brought to the fore. The first of these is "obscene" literature. The law on this subject is exceedingly vague; indeed, if there is to be any law about it, it cannot well help being vague. In practice, anything is obscene which happens to shock a magistrate; and even things which do not shock a magistrate may become the subject of prosecution if they happen to shock some ignorant policeman, as happened recently in the case of the *Decameron*. One of the evils of any law of this sort is that it prevents the diffusion of useful knowledge if such knowledge was not thought useful when the magistrate in question was a boy. Most of us had thought that matters were improving in this respect, but recent experience has made us doubtful. I cannot think that the feeling of shock which an elderly man experiences on being brought in contact with something to which he is not accustomed is a sufficient basis for an accusation of crime.

The second matter in which Mill's principles condemn existing legislation is homosexuality. If two adults voluntarily enter into such a relation, this is a matter which concerns them only, and in which, therefore, the community ought not to intervene. If it were still believed, as it once was, that the toleration of such behavior would expose the community to the fate of Sodom and Gomorrah, the community would have every right to intervene. But it does not acquire a right to intervene merely on the ground that such conduct is thought wicked. The criminal law may rightly be invoked to prevent violence or fraud inflicted upon unwilling victims, but it ought not to be invoked when whatever damage there may be is suffered only by the agents—always assuming that the agents are adults.

Of much greater importance than these remnants of medievalism in our legislation, is the question of unjust power. It was this question which gave rise to the liberalism of the eighteenth and nineteenth centuries. They protested against the power of monarchs, and against the power of the Church in countries where there was religious persecution. They protested also against alien domination wherever there was a strong national sentiment running counter to it. On the whole, these aims were successfully achieved. Monarchs were replaced by presidents, religious persecution almost disappeared, and the Treaty of Versailles did what it could to realize the liberal principle of nationality. In spite of all this, the world did not become a paradise. Lovers of liberty found that there was less of it than there had been, not more. But the slogans and strategies which had brought victory in the past to the liberal cause were not applicable to the new situation, and the liberals found themselves deserted by the supposedly progressive advocates of new forms of tyranny. Kings and priests and capitalists are, on the whole, outmoded bogies. It is officials who represent the modern danger. Against the power of officials, single individuals can do little; only organizations can combat organizations. I think we shall have to revive Montesquieu's doctrine of the division of powers, but in new forms. Consider, for example, the conflict of labor and capital which dominated the minds of Socialists. Socialists imagined that the evils they were combating would cease if the power of capital was put into the hands of the State. This was done in Russia with the approval of organized labor. As soon as it had been done the trade unions were deprived of independent power, and labor found itself more completely enslaved than ever before. There is no monolithic solution of this problem that will leave any loophole for liberty. The only possible solution that a lover of liberty can support must be one in which there are rival powers, neither of them absolute, and each compelled in a crisis to pay some attention to public opinion. This means, in practice, that trade unions must preserve their independence of the executive. Undoubtedly the liberty enjoyed by a man who must belong to his union if he is to obtain employment is an inadequate and imperfect liberty; but it seems to be the best that modern industries can permit.

There is one sphere in which the advocate of liberty is confronted with peculiar difficulties. I mean the sphere of education. It has never been thought that children should be free to choose whether they will be educated or not; and it is not now held that parents ought to have this freedom of choice. Mill thought that the State should insist that children should be educated, but should not itself do the educating. He had, however, not very much to say about how the educating should be done. I will try to consider what he would say on this subject if he were writing now.

Let us begin by asking the question of principle, namely, what should a lover of liberty wish to see done in the schools? I think the ideal but somewhat Utopian answer would be that the pupils should be qualified as far as possible to form a reasonable judgment on controversial questions in regard to which they are likely to have to act. This would require, on the one hand, a training in judicial habits of thought; and, on the other hand, access to impartial supplies of knowledge. In this way the pupil would be prepared for a genuine freedom of choice on becoming adult. We cannot give freedom to the child, but we can give him a preparation for freedom; and this is what education ought to do.

This, however, is not the theory of education which has prevailed in most parts of the world. The theory of education which has prevailed most widely was invented by the Jesuits and perfected by Fichte. Fichte states that the object of education should be to destroy freedom of the will, for why, he asks, should we wish a freedom to choose what is wrong rather than what is right? Fichte knows what is right, and desires a school system such that, when the children grow up, they will be under an inner compulsion to choose what Fichte considers right in preference to what he considers wrong. This theory is adopted in its entirety by Communists and Catholics, and, up to a point, by the State schools of many countries. Its purpose is to produce mental slaves, who have heard only one side on all the burning questions of the day and have been inspired with feelings of horror toward the other side. There is just one slight divergence from what Fichte wanted: although his method of education is approved, the dogmas inculcated differ from country to country and from creed to creed. What Fichte chiefly wished taught was the superiority of the German nation to all others; but on this one small point most of his disciples disagreed with him. The consequence is that State education, in the countries which adopt his principles, produces, in so far as it is successful, a herd of ignorant fanatics, ready at the word of command to engage in war or persecution as may be required of them. So great is this evil that the world would be a better place (at any rate, in my opinion) if State education had never been inaugurated.

There is a broad principle which helps in deciding many questions as to the proper sphere of liberty. The things that make for individual well-being are, broadly speaking, of two sorts: namely, those in which private possession is possible and those in which it is not. The food that one man eats cannot be also eaten by another; but if a man enjoys a poem, he does not thereby place any obstacle in the way of another man's enjoyment of it. Roughly speaking, the goods of which private possession is possible are material, whereas the other sort of goods are mental. Material goods, if the supply is not unlimited, should be distributed on principles of justice: no one should have too much if, in consequence, someone else has too little. This principle of distribution will not result from unrestricted liberty, which would lead to Hobbes's war of all against all and end in the victory of the stronger. But mental goods—such as knowledge, enjoyment of beauty, friendship and love—are not taken away from other people by those whose lives are enriched by them. There is not, therefore, any prima-facie case for restrictions of liberty in this sphere. Those who forbid certain kinds of knowledge, or, like Plato and Stalin, certain kinds of music and poetry, are allowing Government to intervene in regions where it has no *locus standi*. I do not wish to overemphasize the importance of this principle, for there are many cases in which the distinction between material and mental goods cannot be sharply drawn. One of the most obvious of these is the printing of books. A book is as material as a plum pudding, but the good that we expect to derive from it is mental. It is not easy to devise any sound principle upon which even the wisest authority could decide what books deserve to be printed. I do not think that any improvement is possible upon the present diversity of publishers. Wherever there is an authority, whether secular or ecclesiastical, whose permission is required before a book can be printed, the results are disastrous. The same thing applies to the arts: no one, not even a Communist, will now contend that Russian music was improved by Stalin's intervention.

Mill deserved the eminence which he enjoyed in his own day, not by his intellect but by his intellectual virtues. He was not a great philosopher, like Descartes or Hume. In the realm of philosophy, he derived his ideas from Hume and Bentham and his father. But he blended the harshness of the Philosophical Radicals with something of the Romantic Movement, derived first from Coleridge and Carlyle and then from his wife. What he took over, he made rational in assimilating it. The follies and violences of some Romantics made no impression upon him. His intellectual integrity was impeccable. When he engaged in controversy, he did so with the most minutely scrupulous fairness. The people against whom his controversies were directed deserved almost always the urbanely worded strictures which he passed upon them.

In spite of his purely intellectual deficiencies, his influence was very great and very beneficent. He made rationalism and Socialism respectable, though his Socialism was of the pre-Marxist sort which did not involve an increase in the powers of the State. His advocacy of equality for women in the end won almost world-wide acceptance. His book *On Liberty* remains a classic: although it is easy to point out theoretical defects, its value increases as the world travels farther and farther from his teaching. The present world would both astonish and horrify him; but it would be better than it is, if his ethical principles were more respected.

Mind and Matter

PLATO, reinforced by religion, has led mankind to accept the division of the known world into two categories— mind and matter. Physics and psychology alike have begun to throw doubt on this dichotomy. It has begun to seem that matter, like the Cheshire Cat, is becoming gradually diaphanous until nothing of it is left but the grin, caused, presumably, by amusement at those who still think it is there. Mind, on the other hand, under the influence of brain surgery and of the fortunate opportunities provided by war for studying the effects of bullets embedded in cerebral tissue, has begun to appear more and more as a trivial by-product of certain kinds of physiological circumstances. This view has been reinforced by the morbid horror of introspection which besets those who fear that a private life, of no matter what kind, may expose them to the attentions of the police. We have thus a curiously paradoxical situation, reminding one of the duel between Hamlet and Laertes, in which students of physics have become idealists, while many psychologists are on the verge of materialism. The truth is, of course, that mind and matter are, alike, illusions. Physicists, who study matter, discover this fact about matter, psychologists, who study mind, discover this fact about mind. But each remains convinced that the other's subject of study must have some solidity. What I wish to do in this essay is to restate the relations of mind and brain in terms not implying the existence of either.

What one may call the conventional view has altered little since the days of the Cartesians. There is the brain, which acts according to the laws of physics; and there is the mind which, though it seems to have some laws of its own, is in many crucial ways subjected to physical conditions in the brain. The Cartesians supposed a parallelism according to which mind and brain were each determined by its own laws, but the two series were so related that, given an event in the one, it was sure to be accompanied by a corresponding event in the other. To take a simple analogy: suppose an Englishman and a Frenchman recite the Apostles' Creed, one in English, the other in French, at exactly the same speed, you can then, from what one of them is saying at a given moment in his language, infer what the other is saying in his. The two series run parallel, though neither causes the other. Few people would now adhere to this theory in its entirety. The denial of interaction between mind and brain contradicts common sense, and never had any but metaphysical arguments in its favor. We all know that a physical stimulus, such as being hit on the nose, may cause a mental reaction—in this case of pain. And we all know that this mental reaction of pain may be the cause of a physical movement—for example, of the fist. There are, however, two opposing schools, not so much of thought as of practice. One school has as its ideal a complete physical determinism as regards the material universe, combined with a dictionary stating that certain physical occurrences are invariably contemporary with certain mental occurrences. There is another school, of whom the psychoanalysts are the most influential part, which seeks purely psychological laws and does not aim at first establishing a causal skeleton in physics. The difference shows in the interpretation of dreams. If you have a nightmare, the one school will say that it is because you ate too much lobster salad, and the other that it is because you are unconsciously in love with your mother. Far be it from me to take sides in so bitter a debate; my own view would be that each type of explanation is justified where it succeeds. Indeed I should view the whole matter in a way which makes the controversy vanish, but before I can make this clear, there is need of a considerable amount of theoretical clarification.

Descartes, as everybody knows, says "I think, therefore I am," and he goes on at once, as if he had said nothing new, to assert "I am a thing that thinks." It would be difficult to pack so large a number of errors into so few words. To begin with "I think," the word "I" is thrust in to conform with grammar, and grammar embodies the metaphysic of our original Indo-European ancestors as they stammered round their campfires. We must, therefore, cut out the word "I." We will leave the word "think," but without a subject, since the subject embodies a belief in substance which we must shut out of our thoughts. The words "therefore I am" not only repeat the metaphysical sin embodied in the word "I," but commit the further sin, vigorously pilloried throughout the works of Carnap, of confounding a word in inverted commas with a word without inverted commas. When I say "I am," or "Socrates existed," or any similar statement, I am really saying something about the word "I" or the word "Socrates"—roughly speaking, in each case that this word is a name. For it is obvious that, if you think of all the things that there are in the world, they cannot be divided into two classes—namely, those that exist, and those that do not. Non-existence, in fact, is a very rare property. Everybody knows the story of the two German pessimistic philosophers, of whom one exclaimed: "How much happier were it never to have been born." To which the other replied with a sigh: "True! But how few are those who achieve this happy lot." You cannot, in fact, say significantly of anything that it exists. What you can say significantly is that the word denoting it denotes something, which is not true of such a word as "Hamlet." Every statement about Hamlet in the play has implicit the false statement " 'Hamlet' is a name," and that is why you cannot take the play as part of Danish history. So when Descartes says "I am," what he ought to mean is " 'I' is a name"—doubtless a very interesting statement, but not having all the metaphysical consequences which Descartes wishes to draw from it. These, however, are not the mistakes I wish to emphasize in Descartes' philosophy. What I wish to emphasize is the error involved in saying "I am a *thing that thinks*." Here the substance philosophy is assumed. It is assumed that the world consists of more or less permanent objects with changing states. This view was evolved by the original metaphysicians who invented language, and who were much struck by the difference between their enemy in battle and their enemy after he had been slain, although they were persuaded that it was the same person whom they first feared, and then ate. It is from such origins that common sense derives its tenets. And I regret to say that all too many professors of philosophy consider it their duty to be sycophants of common sense, and thus, doubtless unintentionally, to bow down in homage before the savage superstitions of cannibals.

What ought we to substitute for Descartes' belief that he was a thing that thought? There were, of course, two Descartes, the distinction between whom is what gives rise to the problem I wish to discuss. There was Descartes to himself, and Descartes to his friends. He is concerned with what he was to himself. What he was to himself is not best described as a single entity with changing states. The single entity is quite otiose. The changing states suffice. Descartes to himself should have appeared as a series of events, each of which might be called a thought, provided that word is liberally interpreted. What he was to others I will, for the mo-

ment, ignore. It was this series of "thoughts" which consti-
tuted Descartes' "mind," but his mind was no more a separate
entity than the population of New York is a separate entity
over and above the several inhabitants. Instead of saying
"Descartes thinks," we ought to say "Descartes is a series of
which the members are thoughts." And instead of "therefore
Descartes exists," we ought to say "Since 'Descartes' is the
name of this series, it follows that 'Descartes' is a name."
But for the statement "Descartes is a thing which thinks" we
must substitute nothing whatever, since the statement embodies nothing but faulty syntax.

It is time to inquire what we mean by "thoughts" when we
say that Descartes was a series of thoughts. It would be more
conventionally correct to say that Descartes' *mind* was a series
of thoughts, since his body is generally supposed to have been
something different. His mind, we may say, was what Descartes was to himself and to no one else; whereas his body
was public, and appeared to others as well as to himself.
Descartes uses the word "thoughts" somewhat more widely
than it would be used nowadays, and we shall, perhaps, avoid
confusion if we substitute the phrase "mental phenomena."
Before we reach what would ordinarily be called "thinking,"
there are more elementary occurrences, which come under
the heads of "sensation" and "perception." Common sense
would say that perception always has an object, and that in
general the object of perception is not mental. Sensation
and perception would, in common parlance, not count as
"thoughts." Thoughts would consist of such occurrences as
memories, beliefs, and desires. Before considering thoughts in
this narrower sense, I should wish to say a few words about
sensation and perception.

Both "sensation" and "perception" are somewhat confused
concepts, and, as ordinarily defined, it may be doubted

whether either ever occurs. Let us, therefore, in the first instance avoid the use of these words, and try to describe what occurs with as few doubtful assumptions as possible.

It frequently happens that a number of people in the same environment have very similar experiences at approximately the same time. A number of people can hear the same clap of thunder, or the same speech by a politician; and the same people can see the lightning, or the politician thumping the table. We become aware on reflection that there is, in the environment of these people, an event which is not identical with what is heard or seen. There is only one politician, but there is a separate mental occurrence in each of those who see and hear him. In this mental occurrence, psychological analysis distinguishes two elements: one of them is due to those parts of the structure of the individual which he shares with other normal members of his species; the other part embodies results of his past experiences. A certain phrase of the politician evokes in one hearer the reaction "That's put the scoundrels in their place," and in another the quite different reaction, "Never in all my life have I heard such monstrous injustice." Not only such somewhat indirect reactions are different, but often men will actually hear different words because of their prejudices or past experiences. I was present in the House of Lords on an occasion when Keynes felt it necessary to rebuke Lord Beaverbrook for some statistics that the noble journalist had been offering to the House. What Keynes said was: "I have never heard statistics so phony" or "funny." Half the House thought he said "phony," and the other half thought he said "funny." He died almost immediately afterward, leaving the question undecided. No doubt past experience determined which of the two words any given hearer heard. Those who had been much exposed to America heard "phony," while those who had led more shel-

tered lives heard "funny." But in all ordinary cases past experience is concerned much more intimately than in the above
illustration. When you see a solid-looking object, it suggests
tactile images. If you are accustomed to pianos, but not to
gramophones or radio, you will, when you hear piano music,
imagine the hands of the performer on the keys (I have had
this experience, but it is one not open to the young). When
in the morning you smell bacon, gustatory images inevitably
arise. The word "sensation" is supposed to apply to that part
of the mental occurrence which is not due to past individual
experience, while the word "perception" applies to the sensation together with adjuncts that the past history of the individual has rendered inevitable. It is clear that to disentangle
the part of the total experience which is to be called "sensation," is a matter of elaborate psychological theory. What we
know without theory is the total occurrence which is a
"perception."

But the word "perception," as ordinarily used, is question-
begging. Suppose, for example, that I see a chair, or rather
that there is an occurrence which would ordinarily be so
described. The phrase is taken to imply that there is "I"
and there is a chair, and that the perceiving is a relation between the two. I have already dealt with "I," but the chair
belongs to the physical world, which, for the moment, I am
trying to ignore. For the moment I will say only this: common sense supposes that the chair which I perceive would
still be there if I did not perceive it, for example, if I shut
my eyes. Physics and physiology between them assure me
that what is there independently of my seeing, is something
very unlike a visual experience, namely, a mad dance of billions of electrons undergoing billions of quantum transitions.
My relation to this object is indirect, and is known only by
inference; it is not something that I directly experience when-

ever there is that occurrence which I call "seeing a chair."
In fact the whole of what occurs when I have the experience
which I call "seeing a chair" is to be counted as belonging to
my mental world. If there is a chair which is outside my
mental world, as I firmly believe, this is something which is
not a direct object of experience, but is arrived at by a
process of inference. This conclusion has odd consequences.
We must distinguish between the physical world of physics,
and the physical world of our everyday experience. The physical world of physics, supposing physics to be correct, exists
independently of my mental life. From a metaphysical point
of view, it is solid and self-subsistent, always assuming that
there is such a world. Per contra, the physical world of my
everyday experience is a part of my mental life. Unlike the
physical world of physics, it is not solid, and is no more substantial than the world that I see in dreams. On the other hand
it is indubitable, in a way in which the physical world of physics is not. The experience of seeing a chair is one that I cannot explain away. I certainly have this experience, even if I
am dreaming. But the chair of physics, though certainly solid,
perhaps does not exist. It does not exist if I am dreaming.
And even if I am awake it may not exist, if there are fallacies
in certain kinds of inference to which I am prone, but which
are not demonstrative. In short, as Mr. Micawber would say,
the physical world of physics is solid but not indubitable,
while the physical world of daily experience is indubitable
but not solid. In this statement I am using the word "solid"
to mean "existing independently of my mental life."

Let us ask ourselves a very elementary question: What is
the difference between things that happen to sentient beings
and things that happen to lifeless matter? Obviously all sorts
of things happen to lifeless objects. They move and undergo
various transformations, but they do not "experience" these

occurrences whereas we do "experience" things that happen to us. Most philosophers have treated "experience" as something indefinable, of which the meaning is obvious. I regard this as a mistake. I do not think the meaning is obvious, but I also do not think that it is indefinable. What characterizes experience is the influence of past occurrences on present reactions. When you offer a coin to an automatic machine, it reacts precisely as it has done on former occasions. It does not get to know that the offer of a coin means a desire for a ticket, or whatever it may be, and it reacts no more promptly than it did before. The man at the ticket office, on the contrary, learns from experience to react more quickly and to less direct stimuli. This is what leads us to call him intelligent. It is this sort of thing which is the essence of memory. You see a certain person, and he makes a certain remark. The next time you see him you remember the remark. This is essentially analogous to the fact that when you see an object which looks hard, you expect a certain kind of tactile sensation if you touch it. It is this sort of thing that distinguishes an experience from a mere happening. The automatic machine has no experience; the man at the ticket office has experience. This means that a given stimulus produces always the same reaction in the machine, but different reactions in the man. You tell an anecdote, and your hearer replies: "You should have heard how I laughed the first time I heard the story." If, however, you had constructed an automatic machine that would laugh at a joke, it could be relied upon to laugh every time, however often it had heard the joke before. You may, perhaps, find this thought comforting if you are tempted to adopt a materialistic philosophy.

I think it would be just to say that the most essential characteristic of mind is memory, using this word in its broadest sense to include every influence of past experience on present reactions. Memory includes the sort of knowledge which is commonly called knowledge of perception. When you merely see something it can hardly count as knowledge. It becomes knowledge when you say to yourself that you see it, or that there it is. This is a reflection upon the mere seeing. This reflection is knowledge, and because it is possible, the seeing counts as experience and not as a mere occurrence, such as might happen to a stone. The influence of past experience is embodied in the principle of the conditioned reflex, which says that, in suitable circumstances, if A originally produces a certain reaction, and A frequently occurs in conjunction with B, B alone will ultimately produce the reaction that A originally produced. For example: if you wish to teach bears to dance, you place them upon a platform so hot that they cannot bear to leave a foot on it for more than a moment, and meanwhile you play "Rule Britannia" on the orchestra. After a time "Rule Britannia" alone will make them dance. Our intellectual life, even in its highest flights, is based upon this principle.

Like all other distinctions, the distinction between what is living and what is dead is not absolute. There are viruses concerning which specialists cannot make up their minds whether to call them living or dead, and the principle of the conditioned reflex, though characteristic of what is living, finds some exemplification in other spheres. For example: if you unroll a roll of paper, it will roll itself up again as soon as it can. But in spite of such cases, we may take the conditioned reflex as characteristic of life, especially in its higher forms, and above all as characteristic of human intelligence. The relation between mind and matter comes to a head at this point. If the brain is to have any characteristic corresponding to memory, it must be in some way affected by what happens to it, in such a manner as to suggest reproduc-

tion on occasion of a suitable stimulus. This also can be illustrated in a lesser degree by the behavior of inorganic matter. A watercourse which at most times is dry gradually
wears a channel down a gully at the times when it flows, and
subsequent rains follow the course which is reminiscent of
earlier torrents. You may say, if you like, that the river bed
"remembers" previous occasions when it experienced cooling
streams. This would be considered a flight of fancy. You
would say it was a flight of fancy because you are of the
opinion that rivers and river beds do not "think." But if thinking consists of certain modifications of behavior owing to
former occurrences, then we shall have to say that the river
bed thinks, though its thinking is somewhat rudimentary.
You cannot teach it the multiplication table, however wet
the climate may be.

At this point I fear you will be becoming indignant. You
will be inclined to say: "But, my dear Sir, how can you be
so dense? Surely even you must know that thoughts and
pleasures and pains cannot be pushed about like billiard balls,
whereas matter can. Matter occupies space. It is impenetrable;
it is hard (unless it is soft); thoughts are not like this. You
cannot play billiards with your thoughts. When you banish
a thought, the process is quite different from that of being
ejected by the police. You, of course, as a philosopher" (so,
no doubt, you will continue) "are superior to all human
passions. But the rest of us experience pleasures and pains, and
sticks and stones do not. In view of all this I cannot understand how you can be so stupid as to make a mystery of the
difference between mind and matter."

My answer to this consists in saying that I know very much
less than you do about matter. All that I know about matter
is what I can infer by means of certain abstract postulates
about the purely logical attributes of its space-time distribu-

tion. Prima facie, these tell me nothing whatever about its other characteristics. Moreover there are the same reasons for not admitting the concept of substance in the case of matter, as there are in the case of mind. We reduced Descartes' mind to a series of occurrences, and we must do the same for his body. A piece of matter is a series of occurrences bound together by means of certain of the laws of physics. The laws that bind these occurrences together are only approximate and macroscopic. In proper quantum physics, the identity which physical particles preserve in old-fashioned physics disappears. Suppose I want to say: "This is the same chair as it was yesterday." You cannot expect me to tell you accurately what I mean, because it would take volumes to state this correctly. What I mean may be put roughly as follows: classical physics—a system now abandoned—worked with the assumption of particles that persist through time. While this conception lasted, I could maintain that when I said "This is the same chair" I meant "this is composed of the same particles." Before the coming of quantum physics, particles were already out of date, because they involved the concept of substance. But that did not matter so much because it was still possible to define a particle as a certain series of physical occurrences, connected with one another by the law of inertia and other similar principles. Even in the days of the Rutherford-Bohr atom, this point of view could still be maintained. The Rutherford-Bohr atom consisted of a certain number of electrons and protons. The electrons behaved like fleas. They crawled for a while, and then hopped. But an electron was still recognizable after the hops as being the same one that had previously crawled. Now, alas, the atom has suffered atomic disintegration. All that we know about it, even on the most optimistic hypothesis, is that it is a distribution of energy which undergoes various sudden transitions. It is only the transitions of which it is possible to have evidence, for it is only in a transition that energy is radiated, it is only when energy is radiated that our senses are affected, and it is only when our senses are affected that we have evidence as to what has occurred. In the happy days when Bohr was young, we were supposed to know what was going on in the atom in quiet times: there were electrons going round and round the nucleus as planets go round the sun. Now we have to confess to a complete and absolute and eternally ineradicable ignorance as to what the atom does in quiet times. It is as if it were inhabited by newspaper reporters who think nothing worth mentioning except revolutions, so that what happens when no revolution is going on remains wrapped in mystery. On this basis, sameness at different times has completely disappeared. If you want to explain what you mean in physics when you say "This is the same chair as it was yesterday," you must go back to classical physics. You must say: when temperatures are not too high, and chemical circumstances are ordinary, the results obtained by old-fashioned classical physics are more or less right. And when I say that "this is the same chair," I shall mean that old-fashioned physics would say it was the same chair. But I am well aware that this is no more than a convenient and inaccurate way of speaking, and that, in fact, every smallest piece of the chair loses its identity in about one hundred thousandth part of a second. To say that it is the same chair is like saying that the English are the same nation as they were in the time of Queen Elizabeth I, or rather, like what this would be, if many millions of generations had passed since the death of Good Queen Bess.

We have not yet learned to talk about the human brain in the accurate language of quantum physics. Indeed we know too little about it for this language to be necessary. The chief relevance, to our problem, of the mysteries of quantum physics consists in their showing us how very little we know about matter, and, in particular, about human brains. Some physiologists still imagine that they can look through a microscope and see brain tissues. This, of course, is an optimistic delusion. When you think that you look at a chair, you do not see quantum transitions. You have an experience which has a very lengthy and elaborate causal connection with the physical chair, a connection proceeding through photons, rods and cones, and optic nerve to the brain. All these stages are necessary if you are to have the visual experience which is called "seeing the chair." You may stop the photons by closing your eyes, the optic nerve may be severed, or the appropriate part of the brain may be destroyed by a bullet. If any of these things has happened you will not "see the chair." Similar considerations apply to the brain that the physiologist thinks he is examining. There is an experience in him which has a remote causal connection with the brain that he thinks he is seeing. He can only know concerning that brain such elements of structure as will be reproduced in his visual sensation. Concerning properties that are not structural, he can know nothing whatever. He has no right to say that the contents of a brain are different from those of the mind that goes with it. If it is a living brain, he has evidence through testimony and analogy that there is a mind that goes with it. If it is a dead brain, evidence is lacking either way.

I wish to suggest, as a hypothesis which is simple and unifying though not demonstrable, a theory which I prefer to that of correspondence advanced by the Cartesians. We have agreed that mind and matter alike consist of series of events. We have also agreed that we know nothing about the events that make matter, except their space-time structure. What I suggest is that the events that make a living brain are actually identical with those that make the corresponding mind. All the reasons that will naturally occur to you for rejecting this view depend upon confusing material objects with those that you experience in sight and touch. These latter are parts of your mind. I can see, at the moment, if I allow myself to talk the language of common sense, the furniture of my room, the trees waving in the wind, houses, clouds, blue sky, and sun. All these common sense imagines to be outside me. All these I believe to be causally connected with physical objects which are outside me, but as soon as I realize that the physical objects must differ in important ways from what I directly experience, and as soon as I take account of the causal trains that proceed from the physical object to my brain before my sensations occur, I see that from the point of view of physical causation the immediately experienced objects of sense are in my brain and not in the outer world. Kant was right to put the starry heavens and the moral law together, since both were figments of his brain.

If what I am saying is correct, the difference between mind and brain does not consist in the raw material of which they are composed, but in the manner of grouping. A mind and a piece of matter alike are to be considered as groups of events, or rather series of groups of events. The events that are grouped to make a given mind are, according to my theory, the very same events that are grouped to make its brain. Or perhaps it would be more correct to say that they are *some* of the events that make the brain. The important point is, that the difference between mind and brain is not a difference of quality, but a difference of arrangement. It is like the difference between arranging people in geographical order or in alphabetical order, both of which are done in the post office directory. The same people are arranged in both cases, but in quite different contexts. In like manner the context of a visual sensation for physics is physical, and outside the brain.

Going backward, it takes you to the eye, and thence to a photon and thence to a quantum transition in some distant object. The context of the visual sensation for psychology is quite different. Suppose, for example, the visual sensation is that of a telegram saying that you are ruined. A number of events will take place in your mind in accordance with the laws of psychological causation, and it may be quite a long time before there is any purely physical effect, such as tearing your hair, or exclaiming "Woe is me!"

If this theory is right, certain kinds of connection between mind and brain are inescapable. Corresponding to memory, for example, there must be some physical modifying of the brain, and mental life must be connected with physical properties of the brain tissue. In fact, if we had more knowledge, the physical and psychological statements would be seen to be merely different ways of saying the same thing. The ancient question of the dependence of mind on brain, or brain on mind, is thus reduced to linguistic convenience. In cases where we know more about the brain it will be convenient to regard the mind as dependent, but in cases where we know more about the mind it will be convenient to regard the brain as dependent. In either case, the substantial facts are the same, and the difference is only as to the degree of our knowledge.

I do not think it can be laid down absolutely, if the above is right, that there can be no such thing as disembodied mind. There would be disembodied mind if there were groups of events connected according to the laws of psychology, but not according to the laws of physics. We readily believe that dead matter consists of groups of events arranged according to the laws of physics, but not according to the laws of psychology. And there seems no a priori reason why the opposite should not occur. We can say we have no empirical evidence of it, but more than this we cannot say.

Experience has shown me that the theory which I have been trying to set forth is one which people are very apt to misunderstand, and, as misunderstood, it becomes absurd. I will therefore recapitulate its main points in the hope that by means of new wording they may become less obscure.

First: the world is composed of events, not of things with changing states, or rather, everything that we have a right to say about the world can be said on the assumption that there are only events and not things. Things, as opposed to events, are an unnecessary hypothesis. This part of what I have to say is not exactly new, since it was said by Heraclitus. His view, however, annoyed Plato and has therefore ever since been considered not quite gentlemanly. In these democratic days this consideration need not frighten us. Two kinds of supposed entities are dissolved if we adopt the view of Heraclitus: on the one hand, persons, and on the other hand, material objects. Grammar suggests that you and I are more or less permanent entities with changing states, but the permanent entities are unnecessary, and the changing states suffice for saying all that we know on the matter. Exactly the same sort of thing applies to physical objects. If you go into a shop and buy a loaf of bread, you think that you have bought a "thing" which you can bring home with you. What you have in fact bought is a series of occurrences linked together by certain causal laws.

Second: sensible objects, as immediately experienced, that is to say, what we see when we see chairs and tables and the sun and the moon and so on, are parts of our minds and are not either the whole or part of the physical objects that we think we are seeing. This part of what I am saying is also not new. It comes from Berkeley, as reinforced by Hume. The arguments that I should use for it, however, are not exactly Berkeley's. I should point out that if a number of people look at a single object from different points of view, their visual impressions differ according to the laws of perspective and according to the way the light falls. Therefore no one of the visual impressions is that neutral "thing" which all think they are seeing. I should point out also that physics leads us to believe in causal chains, starting from objects and reaching our sense organs, and that it would be very odd if the last link in this causal chain were exactly like the first.

Third: I should admit that there *may* be no such thing as a physical world distinct from my experiences, but I should point out that if the inferences which lead to matter are rejected, I ought also to reject the inferences which lead me to believe in my own mental past. I should point out further that no one sincerely rejects beliefs which only such inferences can justify. I therefore take it that there are events which I do not experience, although some things about some of these can be inferred from what I do experience. Except where mental phenomena are concerned, the inferences that I can make as to the external causes of my experiences are only as to structure, not as to quality. The inferences that are warranted are those to be found in theoretical physics; they are abstract and mathematical and give no indication whatever as to the intrinsic character of physical objects.

Fourth: if the foregoing is accepted there must be two sorts of space, one the sort of space which is known through experience, especially in my visual field, the other the sort of space that occurs in physics, which is known only by inference and is bound up with causal laws. Failure to distinguish these two kinds of space is a source of much confusion. I will take again the case of a physiologist who is examining someone else's brain. Common sense supposes that he sees that brain and that what he sees is matter. Since what he sees is obviously quite different from what is being thought by the patient whom he is examining, people conclude that mind and matter are quite different things. Matter is what the physiologist sees, mind is what the patient is thinking. But this whole order of ideas, if I am right, is a mass of confusions. What the physiologist sees, if we mean by this something that he experiences, is an event in his own mind and has only an elaborate causal connection with the brain that he imagines himself to be seeing. This is obvious as soon as we think of physics. In the brain that he thinks he is seeing there are quantum transitions. These lead to emission of photons, the photons travel across the intervening space and hit the eye of the physiologist. They then cause complicated occurrences in the rods and cones, and a disturbance which travels along the optic nerve to the brain. When this disturbance reaches the brain, the physiologist has the experience which is called "seeing the other man's brain." If anything interferes with the causal chain, e.g. because the other man's brain is in darkness, because the physiologist has closed his eyes, because the physiologist is blind, or because he has a bullet in the brain at the optic center, he does not have the experience called "seeing the other man's brain." Nor does the event occur at the same time as what he thinks he sees. In the case of terrestrial objects, the difference of time is negligible, but in the case of celestial objects it may be very large, even as much as millions of years. The relation of a visual experience to the physical object that common sense thinks it is seeing is thus indirect and causal, and there is no reason to suppose that close similarity between them that common sense imagines to exist. All this is connected with the two kinds of space that I wrote of a moment ago. I horrified all the philosophers by saying that their thoughts were in their heads. With one voice they assured me that they had no thoughts in their heads whatever, but politeness forbids me to accept this assurance.

Perhaps, however, it might be well to explain exactly what I mean, since the remark is elliptical. Stated accurately, what I mean is as follows: physical space, unlike the space of perception, is based upon causal contiguity. The causal contiguities of sense perceptions are with the physical stimuli immediately preceding them and with the physical reactions immediately following them. Precise location in physical space belongs not to single events but to such groups of events as physics would regard as a momentary state of a piece of matter, if it indulged in such old-fashioned language. A thought is one of a group of events, such as will count for purposes of physics as a region in the brain. To say that a thought is in the brain is an abbreviation for the following: a thought is one of a group of compresent events, which group is a region in the brain. I am not suggesting that thoughts are in psychological space, except in the case of sense impressions (if these are to be called "thoughts").

Fifth: a piece of matter is a group of events connected by causal laws, namely, the causal laws of physics. A mind is a group of events connected by causal laws, namely, the causal laws of psychology. An event is not rendered either mental or material by any intrinsic quality, but only by its causal relations. It is perfectly possible for an event to have both the causal relations characteristic of physics and those characteristic of psychology. In that case, the event is both mental and material at once. There is no more difficulty about this than there is about a man being at once a baker and a father. Since we know nothing about the intrinsic quality of physical events except when these are mental events that we directly experience, we cannot say either that the physical world outside our heads is different from the mental world or that it is not. The supposed problem of the relations of mind and matter arises only through mistakenly treating both as "things" and not as groups of events. With the theory that I have been suggesting, the whole problem vanishes.

In favor of the theory that I have been advocating, the most important thing to be said is that it removes a mystery. Mystery is always annoying, and is usually due to lack of clear analysis. The relations of mind and matter have puzzled people for a long time, but if I am right they need puzzle people no longer.

The Cult of "Common Usage"

THE most influential school of philosophy in Britain at the present day maintains a certain linguistic doctrine to which I am unable to subscribe. I do not wish to misrepresent this school, but I suppose any opponent of any doctrine is thought to misrepresent it by those who hold it. The doctrine, as I understand it, consists in maintaining that the language of daily life, with words used in their ordinary meanings, suffices for philosophy, which has no need of technical terms or of changes in the signification of common terms. I find myself totally unable to accept this view. I object to it:

(1) Because it is insincere;

(2) Because it is capable of excusing ignorance of mathematics, physics, and neurology in those who have had only a classical education;

(3) Because it is advanced by some in a tone of unctuous rectitude, as if opposition to it were a sin against democracy;

(4) Because it makes philosophy trivial;

(5) Because it makes almost inevitable the perpetuation among philosophers of the muddle-headedness they have taken over from common sense.

(1). *Insincerity*. I will illustrate this by a fable. The Professor of Mental Philosophy, when called by his bedmaker one morning, developed a dangerous frenzy, and had to be taken away by the police in an ambulance. I heard a colleague, a believer in "common usage," asking the poor philosopher's doctor about the occurrence. The doctor replied that the professor had had an attack of temporary psychotic instability, which had subsided after an hour. The believer in "common usage," so far from objecting to the doctor's language, repeated it to other inquirers. But it happened that I, who live on the professor's staircase, overheard the following dialogue between the bedmaker and the policeman:

Policeman. 'Ere, I want a word with yer.

Bedmaker. What do you mean—"A word"? I ain't done nothing.

Policeman. Ah, that's just it. Yer ought to 'ave done something. Couldn't yer see the pore gentleman was mental?

Bedmaker. That I could. For an 'ole *hour* 'e went on something chronic. But when they're mental you can't make them understand.

In this little dialogue, "word," "mean," "mental," and "chronic" are all used in accordance with common usage. They are not so used in the pages of "Mind" by those who pretend that common usage is what they believe in. What in fact they believe in is not common usage, as determined by mass observation, statistics, medians, standard deviations, and the rest of the apparatus. What they believe in is the usage of persons who have their amount of education, neither more nor less. Less is illiteracy, more is pedantry—so we are given to understand.

(2). *An excuse for ignorance.* Every motorist is accustomed to speedometers and accelerators, but unless he has learned mathematics he attaches no precise significance to "speed" or "acceleration." If he does attach a precise significance to these words, he will know that his speed and his acceleration are at every moment unknowable, and that, if he is fined for speeding, the conviction must be based on insufficient evidence if the time when he is supposed to have speeded is mentioned. On these grounds I will agree with the advocate of common usage that such a word as "speed," if used in daily life, must be used as in daily life, and not as in mathematics. But then it should be realized that "speed" is a vague notion, and that equal truth may attach to all three of the statements in the conjugation of the following irregular verb:

"I was at rest" (motorist).

"You were moving at 20 miles an hour" (a friend).

"He was traveling at 60 miles an hour" (the police).

It is because this state of affairs is puzzling to magistrates that mathematicians have abandoned common usage.

(3). Those who advocate common usage in philosophy sometimes speak in a manner that suggests the *mystique* of the "common man." They may admit that in organic chemistry there is need of long words, and that quantum physics requires formulas that are difficult to translate into ordinary English, but philosophy (they think) is different. It is not the function of philosophy—so they maintain—to teach something that uneducated people do not know; on the contrary, its function is to teach superior persons that they are not as superior as they thought they were, and that those who are *really* superior can show their skill by making sense of common sense.

It is, of course, a dreadful thing in these days to lay claim to any kind of superiority except in athletics, movies, and money-making. Nevertheless I will venture to say that in former centuries common sense made what we now think mistakes. It used to be thought that there could not be people at the antipodes, because they would fall off, or, if they avoided that, they would grow dizzy from standing on their heads. It used to be thought absurd to say that the earth rotates, because everybody can see that it doesn't. When it was first suggested that the sun may be as large as the Peloponnesus, common sense was outraged. But all this was long ago. I do not know at what date common sense became all-wise. Perhaps it was in 1776; perhaps in 1848; or perhaps with the passing of the Education Act in 1870. Or perhaps it was only when physiologists such as Adrian and Sherrington began to make scientific inroads on philosophers' ideas about perception.

(4). Philosophy, as conceived by the school I am discussing, seems to me a trivial and uninteresting pursuit. To discuss endlessly what silly people mean when they say silly things may be amusing but can hardly be important. Does the full moon look as large as a half-crown or as large as a soup plate? Either answer can be proved correct by experiment. It follows that there is an ambiguity in the question. A modern philosopher will clear up the ambiguity for you with meticulous care.

But let us take an example which is less unfair, say the question of immortality. Orthodox Christianity asserts that we survive death. What does it mean by this assertion? And in what sense, if any, is the assertion true? The philosophers with whom I am concerned will consider the first of these questions, but will say that the second is none of their business. I agree entirely that, in this case, a discussion as to what is meant is important and highly necessary as a preliminary to a consideration of the substantial question, but if nothing can be said on the substantial question, it seems a waste of time to discuss what it means. These philosophers remind me of the shopkeeper of whom I once asked the shortest way to Winchester. He called to a man in the back premises:

"Gentleman wants to know the shortest way to Winchester."

"Winchester?" an unseen voice replied.

"Aye."

"Way to Winchester?"

"Aye."

"Shortest way?"

"Aye."

"Dunno."

He wanted to get the nature of the question clear, but took no interest in answering it. This is exactly what modern philosophy does for the earnest seeker after truth. Is it surprising that young people turn to other studies?

(5). Common sense, though all very well for everyday purposes, is easily confused, even by such simple questions as "Where is the rainbow?" When you hear a voice on a gramophone record, are you hearing the man who spoke or a reproduction? When you feel a pain in a leg that has been amputated, where is the pain? If you say it is in your head, would it be in your head if the leg had not been amputated? If you say yes, then what reason have you ever for thinking you have a leg? And so on.

No one wants to alter the language of common sense, any more than we wish to give up talking of the sun rising and setting. But astronomers find a different language better, and I contend that a different language is better in philosophy.

Let us take an example. A philosophy containing such a large linguistic element cannot object to the question: What is meant by the word "word"? But I do not see how this is to be answered within the vocabulary of common sense. Let us take the word "cat," and for the sake of definiteness let us take the written word. Clearly there are many instances of the word, no one of which *is* the word. If I say "Let us discuss the word 'cat,' " the word "cat" does not occur in what I say, but only an instance of the word. The word itself is no part of the sensible world; if it is anything, it is an eternal supersensible entity in a Platonic heaven. The word, we may say, is a class of similar shapes, and, like all classes, is a logical fiction.

But our difficulties are not at an end. Similarity is neither necessary nor sufficient to make a shape a member of the class which is the word "cat." The word may be written in capitals or in small letters, legibly or illegibly, in black on a white ground or in white on a blackboard. If I write the word "catastrophe," the first three letters do not constitute an instance of the word "cat." The most necessary thing in an instance of the word is *intention*. If a piece of marble happened to have a vein making the shape "cat" we should not think this an instance of the word.

It thus appears that we cannot define the word "word" without (*a*) a logical theory of classes, and (*b*) a psychological understanding of intention. These are difficult matters. I conclude that common sense, whether correct or incorrect in the use of words, does not know in the least what words are—I wish I could believe that this conclusion would render it speechless.

Let us take another problem, that of perception. There is here an admixture of philosophical and scientific questions, but this admixture is inevitable in many questions, or, if not inevitable, can only be avoided by confining ourselves to comparatively unimportant aspects of the matter in hand.

Here is a series of questions and answers.

Q. When I see a table, will what I see be still there if I shut my eyes?

A. That depends upon the sense in which you use the word "see."

Q. What is still there when I shut my eyes?

A. This is an empirical question. Don't bother me with it, but ask the physicists.

Q. What exists when my eyes are open, but not when they are shut?

A. This again is empirical, but in deference to previous philosophers I will answer you: colored surfaces.

Q. May I infer that there are two senses of "see"? In the first, when I "see" a table, I "see" something conjectural about which physics has vague notions that are probably wrong. In the second, I "see" colored surfaces which cease to exist when I shut my eyes.

A. That is correct if you want to think clearly, but our philosophy makes clear thinking unnecessary. By oscillating between the two meanings, we avoid paradox and shock, which is more than most philosophers do.

Knowledge and Wisdom

MOST people would agree that, although our age far surpasses all previous ages in knowledge, there has been no correlative increase in wisdom. But agreement ceases as soon as we attempt to define "wisdom" and consider means of promoting it. I want to ask first what wisdom is, and then what can be done to teach it.

There are, I think, several factors that contribute to wisdom. Of these I should put first a sense of proportion: the capacity to take account of all the important factors in a problem and to attach to each its due weight. This has become more difficult than it used to be owing to the extent and complexity of the specialized knowledge required of various kinds of technicians. Suppose, for example, that you are engaged in research in scientific medicine. The work is difficult and is likely to absorb the whole of your intellectual energy. You have not time to consider the effect which your discoveries or inventions may have outside the field of medicine. You succeed (let us say), as modern medicine has succeeded, in enormously lowering the infant death rate, not only in Europe and America, but also in Asia and Africa. This has the entirely unintended result of making the food supply inadequate and lowering the standard of life in the most populous parts of the world. To take an even more spectacular example, which is in everybody's mind at the present time: You study the composition of the atom from a disinterested desire for knowledge, and incidentally place in the hands of powerful lunatics the means of destroying the human race. In such ways the pursuit of knowledge may become harmful unless it is combined with wisdom; and wisdom in the sense of comprehensive vision is not necessarily present in specialists in the pursuit of knowledge.

Comprehensiveness alone, however, is not enough to constitute wisdom. There must be, also, a certain awareness of the ends of human life. This may be illustrated by the study of history. Many eminent historians have done more harm than good because they viewed facts through the distorting medium of their own passions. Hegel had a philosophy of history which did not suffer from any lack of comprehensiveness, since it started from the earliest times and continued into an indefinite future. But the chief lesson of history which he sought to inculcate was that from the year A.D. 400 down to his own time Germany had been the most important nation and the standard bearer of progress in the world. Perhaps one could stretch the comprehensiveness that constitutes wisdom to include not only intellect but also feeling. It is by no means uncommon to find men whose knowledge is wide but whose feelings are narrow. Such men lack what I am calling wisdom.

It is not only in public ways, but in private life equally, that wisdom is needed. It is needed in the choice of ends to be pursued and in emancipation from personal prejudice. Even an end which it would be noble to pursue if it were attainable may be pursued unwisely if it is inherently impossible of achievement. Many men in past ages devoted their lives to a search for the philosopher's stone and the elixir of life. No doubt, if they could have found them, they would have conferred great benefits upon mankind, but as it was their lives were wasted. To descend to less heroic matters, consider the case of two men, Mr. A and Mr. B, who hate each other and, through mutual hatred, bring each other to destruction. Sup-

pose you go to Mr. A and say, "Why do you hate Mr. B?"
He will no doubt give you an appalling list of Mr. B's vices,
partly true, partly false. And now suppose you go to Mr. B.
He will give you an exactly similar list of Mr. A's vices with
an equal admixture of truth and falsehood. Suppose you now
come back to Mr. A and say, "You will be surprised to learn
that Mr. B says the same things about you as you say about
him," and you go to Mr. B and make a similar speech. The
first effect, no doubt, will be to increase their mutual hatred,
since each will be so horrified by the other's injustice. But
perhaps, if you have sufficient patience and sufficient persuasiveness, you may succeed in convincing each that the other
has only the normal share of human wickedness, and that their
enmity is harmful to both. If you can do this, you will have
instilled some fragment of wisdom.

I think the essence of wisdom is emancipation, as far as possible, from the tyranny of the here and the now. We cannot
help the egoism of our senses. Sight and sound and touch are
bound up with our own bodies and cannot be made impersonal. Our emotions start similarly from ourselves. An infant
feels hunger or discomfort, and is unaffected except by his own
physical condition. Gradually with the years, his horizon
widens, and, in proportion as his thoughts and feelings become
less personal and less concerned with his own physical states,
he achieves growing wisdom. This is of course a matter of degree. No one can view the world with complete impartiality;
and if anyone could, he would hardly be able to remain alive.
But it is possible to make a continual approach toward impartiality, on the one hand, by knowing things somewhat remote in time or space, and, on the other hand, by giving to
such things their due weight in our feelings. It is this approach
toward impartiality that constitutes growth in wisdom.

Can wisdom in this sense be taught? And, if it can, should

the teaching of it be one of the aims of education? I should answer both these questions in the affirmative. We are told on Sundays that we should love our neighbor as ourselves. On the other six days of the week, we are exhorted to hate him. You may say that this is nonsense, since it is not our neighbor whom we are exhorted to hate. But you will remember that the precept was exemplified by saying that the Samaritan was our neighbor. We no longer have any wish to hate Samaritans and so we are apt to miss the point of the parable. If you want to get its point, you should substitute Communist or anti-Communist, as the case may be, for Samaritan. It might be objected that it is right to hate those who do harm. I do not think so. If you hate them, it is only too likely that you will become equally harmful; and it is very unlikely that you will induce them to abandon their evil ways. Hatred of evil is itself a kind of bondage to evil. The way out is through understanding, not through hate. I am not advocating non-resistance. But I am saying that resistance, if it is to be effective in preventing the spread of evil, should be combined with the greatest degree of understanding and the smallest degree of force that is compatible with the survival of the good things that we wish to preserve.

It is commonly urged that a point of view such as I have been advocating is incompatible with vigor in action. I do not think history bears out this view. Queen Elizabeth I in England and Henri IV in France lived in a world where almost everybody was fanatical, either on the Protestant or on the Catholic side. Both remained free from the errors of their time and both, by remaining free, were beneficent and certainly not ineffective. Abraham Lincoln conducted a great war without ever departing from what I have been calling wisdom.

I have said that in some degree wisdom can be taught. I think that this teaching should have a larger intellectual element than has been customary in what has been thought of as moral instruction. I think that the disastrous results of hatred and narrow-mindedness to those who feel them can be pointed out incidentally in the course of giving knowledge. I do not think that knowledge and morals ought to be too much separated. It is true that the kind of specialized knowledge which is required for various kinds of skill has very little to do with wisdom. But it should be supplemented in education by wider surveys calculated to put it in its place in the total of human activities. Even the best technicians should also be good citizens; and when I say "citizens," I mean citizens of the world and not of this or that sect or nation. With every increase of knowledge and skill, wisdom becomes more necessary, for every such increase augments our capacity of realizing our purposes, and therefore augments our capacity for evil, if our purposes are unwise. The world needs wisdom as it has never needed it before; and if knowledge continues to increase, the world will need wisdom in the future even more than it does now.

A Philosophy for Our Time

ALTHOUGH this is my subject I do not think that the tasks of philosophy in our time are in any way different from its tasks at other times. Philosophy has, I believe, a certain perennial value, which is unchanging except in one respect: that some ages depart from wisdom more widely than others do, and have, therefore, more need of philosophy combined with less willingness to accept it. Our age is in many respects one which has little wisdom, and which would therefore profit greatly by what philosophy has to teach.

The value of philosophy is partly in relation to thought and partly in relation to feeling, though its effects in these two ways are closely interconnected. On the theoretical side it is a help in understanding the universe as a whole, in so far as this is possible. On the side of feeling it is a help toward a just appreciation of the ends of human life. I propose to consider first what philosophy can do for our thoughts, and then what it can do for our feelings.

The Here and the Now

The first thing that philosophy does, or should do, is to enlarge intellectual imagination. Animals, including human beings, view the world from a center consisting of the here and the now. Our senses, like a candle in the night, spread a gradually diminishing illumination upon objects as they become more distant. But we never get away from the fact that in our animal life we are compelled to view everything from just one standpoint.

Science attempts to escape from this geographical and chronological prison. In physics the origin of co-ordinates in space-time is wholly arbitrary, and the physicist aims at saying things which have nothing to do with his point of view but would be equally true for an inhabitant of Sirius or of an extra-galactic nebula.

Here again there are stages in emancipation. History and geology take us away from the now, astronomy takes us away from the here. The man whose mind has been filled with these studies gets a feeling that there is something accidental, and almost trivial, about the fact that his ego occupies a very particular portion of the space-time stream. His intellect becomes gradually more and more detached from these physical needs. It acquires in this way a generality and scope and power which is impossible to one whose thoughts are bounded by his animal wants.

Up to a point this is recognized in all civilized countries. A learned man is not expected to grow his own food and is relieved to a considerable extent of the useless expenditure of time and worry on the mere problem of keeping alive. It is, of course, only through this social mechanism that an impersonal outlook is in any degree possible. We all become absorbed in our animal wants in so far as is necessary for survival, but it has been found useful that men with certain kinds of capacity should be free to develop a way of thinking and feeling which is not bounded by their own need. This is done to some extent by the acquisition of any branch of knowledge, but it is done most completely by the sort of general survey that is characteristic of philosophy.

Different Pictures of the Universe

If you read the systems of the great philosophers of the past you will find that there are a number of different pictures of the universe which have seemed good to men with a certain kind of imagination. Some have thought that there is nothing in the world but mind, that physical objects are really phantoms. Others have thought that there is nothing but matter, and that what we call "mind" is only an odd way in which certain kinds of matter behave. I am not at the moment concerned to say that any one of these ways of viewing the world is more true or otherwise more desirable than another. What I am concerned to say is that practice in appreciating these different world pictures stretches the mind and makes it more receptive of new and perhaps fruitful hypotheses.

There is another intellectual use which philosophy ought to have, though in this respect it not infrequently fails. It ought to inculcate a realization of human fallibility and of the uncertainty of many things which to the uneducated seem indubitable. Children at first will refuse to believe that the earth is round and will assert passionately that they can see that it is flat.

But the more important applications of the kind of uncertainty that I have in mind are in regard to such things as social systems and theologies. When we have acquired the habit of impersonal thinking we shall be able to view the popular beliefs of our own nation, our own class, or our own religious sect with the same detachment with which we view those of others. We shall discover that the beliefs that are held most firmly and most passionately are very often those for which there is least evidence. When one large body of men believes A, and another large body of men believes B, there is a tendency of each body to hate the other for believing anything so obviously absurd.

The best cure for this tendency is the practice of going by the evidence, and forgoing certainty where evidence is lacking. This applies not only to theological and political beliefs but also to social customs. The study of anthropology shows that an amazing variety of social customs exists, and that societies can persist with habits that might be thought contrary to human nature. This kind of knowledge is very valuable as an antidote to dogmatism, especially in our own day when rival dogmatisms are the chief danger that threatens mankind.

Closely parallel to the development of impersonal thought there is the development of impersonal feeling, which is at least equally important and which ought equally to result from a philosophical outlook. Our desires, like our senses, are primarily self-centered. The egocentric character of our desires interferes with our ethics. In the one case, as in the other, what is to be aimed at is not a complete absence of the animal equipment that is necessary for life but the addition to it of something wider, more general, and less bound up with personal circumstances. We should not admire a parent who had no more affection for his own children than for those of others, but we should admire a man who from love of his own children is led to a general benevolence. We should not admire a man, if such a man there were, who was so indifferent to food as to become undernourished, but we should admire the man who from knowledge of his own need of food is led to a general sympathy with the hungry.

What philosophy should do in matters of feeling is very closely analogous to what it should do in matters of thought. It should not subtract from the personal life but should add to it. Just as the philosopher's intellectual survey is wider than that of an uneducated man, so also the scope of his desires and interests should be wider. Buddha is said to have asserted that he could not be happy so long as even one human being was suffering. This is carrying things to an extreme and, if taken literally, would be excessive, but it illustrates that universalizing of feeling of which I am speaking. A man who has acquired a philosophical way of feeling, and not only of thinking, will note what things seem to him good and bad in his own experience, and will wish to secure the former and avoid the latter for others as well as for himself.

Roots of Social Progress

Ethics, like science, should be general and should be emancipated, as far as this is humanly possible, from tyranny of the here and now. There is a simple rule by which ethical maxims can be tested, and it is this: "No ethical maxim must contain a proper name." I mean by a proper name any designation of a particular part of space-time; not only the names of individual people but also the names of regions, countries, and historical periods. And when I say that ethical maxims should have this character I am suggesting something more than a cold intellectual assent, for, so long as that is all, a maxim may have very little influence on conduct. I mean something more active, something in the nature of actual desire or impulse, something which has its root in sympathetic imagination. It is from feelings of this generalized sort that most social progress has sprung and must still spring. If your hopes and wishes are confined to yourself, or your family, or your nation, or your class, or the adherents of your creed, vou will find that all your affections and all your kindly feelings are paralleled by dislikes and hostile sentiments. From such a duality in men's feelings spring almost all the major evils in human life—cruelties, oppressions, persecutions, and wars. If our world is to escape the disasters which threaten it men must learn to be less circumscribed in their sympathies.

This has no doubt always been true in a measure but it is more true now than it ever was before. Mankind, owing to science and scientific technique, are unified for evil but are not yet unified for good. They have learned the technique of world-wide mutual destruction but not the more desirable technique of world-wide co-operation. The failure to learn this more desirable technique has its source in emotional limitations, in the confining of sympathy to one's own group, and in indulgence in hatred and fear toward other groups.

World-wide co-operation with our present technique could abolish poverty and war, and could bring to all mankind a level of happiness and well-being such as has never hitherto existed. But although this is obvious men still prefer to confine co-operation to their own groups and to indulge toward other groups a fierce hostility which fills daily life with terrifying visions of disaster. The reasons for this absurd and tragic inability to behave as everybody's interests would dictate lie not in anything external but in our own emotional nature. If we could feel in our moments of vision as impersonally as a man of science can think, we should see the folly of our divisions and contests, and we should soon perceive that our own interests are compatible with those of others but are not compatible with the desire to bring others to ruin. Fanatical dogmatism, which is one of the great evils of our time, is primarily an intellectual defect and, as I suggested before, it is one to which philosophy supplies an intellectual antidote. But a great deal of dogmatism has also an emotional source: namely, fear. It is felt that only the closest social unity is adequate to meet the enemy and that the slightest deviation from orthodoxy will have a weakening effect in war. Frightened populations are intolerant populations. I do not think they are wise in this. Fear seldom inspires rational action and very often inspires action which increases the very danger that is feared.

This certainly is the case with the irrational dogmatism that has been spreading over large parts of the world. Where danger is real the impersonal kind of feeling that philosophy should generate is the best cure. Spinoza, who was perhaps the best example of the way of feeling of which I am speaking, remained completely calm at all times, and in the last day of his life preserved the same friendly interest in others as he had shown in days of health. To a man whose hopes and wishes extend widely beyond his personal life there is not the same occasion for fear that there is for a man of more limited desires. He can reflect that when he is dead there will be others to carry on his work and that even the greatest disasters of past times have sooner or later been overcome. He can see the human race as a unity and history as a gradual emergence from animal subjection to nature. It is easier for him than it would be if he had no philosophy to avoid frantic panic and to develop a capacity for stoic endurance in misfortune. I do not pretend that such a man will always be happy. It is scarcely possible to be always happy in a world such as that in which we find ourselves, but I do think that the true philosopher is less likely than others are to suffer from baffled despair and fascinated terror in the contemplation of possible disaster.

A Plea for Clear Thinking

Words have two functions: on the one hand to state facts, and on the other to evoke emotions. The latter is their older function, and is performed among animals by cries which antedate language. One of the most important elements in the transition from barbarism to civilization is the increasing use of words to indicate rather than to excite, but in politics little has been done in this direction. If I say the area of Hungary is so many square kilometers, I am making a purely informative statement, but when I say that the area of the U.S.S.R. is one sixth of the land surface of the globe, my statement is mainly emotional.

The Meaning of "Democracy"

All the stock words of political controversy, in spite of having a definite dictionary meaning, have in use meanings which differ according to the political affiliation of the speaker, and agree only in their power of rousing violent emotions. The word "liberty" originally meant chiefly absence of alien domination; then it came to mean restrictions of royal power; then, in the days of the "rights of man," it came to denote various respects in which it was thought that each individual should be free from governmental interference; and then at last, in the hands of Hegel, it came to be "true liberty," which amounted to little more than gracious permission to obey the police. In our day, the word "democracy" is going through a similar transformation: it used to mean government by a majority, with a somewhat undefined modicum of personal freedom; it then came to mean the aims of the political party that represented the interests of the poor, on the ground that the poor everywhere are the majority. At the next stage it represented the aims of the leaders of that party. It has now come, throughout Eastern Europe and a large part of Asia, to mean despotic government by those who were in some former time champions of the poor, but who now confine such championship exclusively to inflicting ruin upon the rich, except when the rich are "democratic" in the new sense. This is a very potent and successful method of political agitation. Men who have long heard a certain word with a certain emotion are apt to feel the same emotion when they hear the same word, even if its meaning is changed. If, some years hence, volunteers are required for a trial journey to the moon, they will be more easily obtained if that satellite is rechristened "home sweet home."

It should be a part of education, as it is of science and scientific philosophy, to teach the young to use words with a precise meaning, rather than with a vague mist of emotion. I know from observation that the pursuit of scientific philosophy is practically effective in this respect. Two or three years before the outbreak of the late war I attended an international congress of scientific philosophy in Paris. Those who attended belonged to a great variety of nations, and their governments were engaged in acrimonious disputes which it seemed practically hopeless to settle except by force. The members of the congress in their professional hours discussed abstruse points of logic or theory of knowledge, apparently wholly divorced from the world of affairs, but in their unprofessional moments they debated all the most vexed questions of international politics. Not once did I hear any of them display patriotic bias or fail through passion to give due weight to arguments adverse to his national interest. If that congress could have taken over the government of the world, and been protected by Martians from the fury of all the fanatics whom they would have outraged, they could have come to just decisions without being compelled to ignore the protests of indignant minorities among themselves. If the governments of their several countries had so chosen, they could have educated the young to an equal degree of impartiality. But they did not so choose. Governments in their schools are only too ready to foster the germs of irrationality, hatred, suspicion and envy, which are all too easily fructified in human minds.

Political passion is so virulent and so natural to man that the accurate use of language cannot well be first taught in the political sphere; it is easier to begin with words that arouse comparatively little passion. The first effect of a training in intellectual neutrality is apt to look like cynicism. Take, say, the word "truth," a word which some people use with awe, and others, like Pontius Pilate, with derision. It produces a shock when the learner first hears such a statement as "truth is a property of sentences," because he is accustomed to think of sentences neither as grand nor as ridiculous. Or take again the word "infinity"; people will tell you that a finite mind cannot comprehend the infinite, but if you ask them "what do you mean by 'infinite,' and in what sense is a human mind finite?" they will at once lose their tempers. In fact, the word "infinite" has a perfectly precise meaning which has been assigned to it by the mathematicians, and which is quite as comprehensible as anything else in mathematics.

Experience in the technique of taking the emotion out of words and substituting a clear logical significance will stand a man in good stead if he wishes to keep his head amid the welter of excited propaganda. In 1917, Wilson proclaimed the great principle of self-determination, according to which every nation had a right to direct its own affairs; but unfortunately he forgot to append the definition of the word "nation." Was Ireland a nation? Yes, certainly. Was northeast Ulster a nation? Protestants said yes, and Catholics said no, and the dictionary was silent. To this day this question remains undecided, and the controversies in regard to it are liable to influence the policy of the United States toward Great Britain. In Petrograd, as it then was, during the time of Kerensky, a certain single house proclaimed itself a nation rightly struggling to be free, and appealed to President Wilson to give it a separate Parliament. This, however, was felt to be going too far. If President Wilson had been trained in logical accuracy he would have appended a footnote saying that a nation must contain not less than some assigned number of individuals. This, however, would have made his principle arbitrary and would have robbed it of rhetorical force.

Translating Problems into an Abstract Form

One useful technique which scientific philosophy teaches consists in the transformation of every problem from a concrete to an abstract form. Take, for example, the following: Had the Irish the right to object to being included with Great Britain in one democratic government? Every American Radical would say yes. Have the Moslems the same right as against the Hindus? Nine out of ten American Radicals would formerly have said no. I do not suggest that either of these problems can be solved by being stated in abstract terms, but I do say that, when for the two concrete problems we substitute a single abstract problem in which the letters A and B replace the names of nations or communities about which we have strong feelings, it becomes very much easier to see what sort of considerations ought to be involved in arriving at any impartial solution.

Political problems cannot be solved either by correct thinking alone, or by right feeling alone: correct thinking can contribute neutrality in the estimation of facts, but right feeling is needed to give dynamic force to knowledge. Unless a wish for the general welfare exists, no amount of knowledge will inspire action calculated to promote the happiness of mankind. But many men, owing to confused thinking, can act under the direction of bad passions without any realization that they are doing so, and when, by purely intellectual means, this realization is brought home to them, they can often be induced to act in a manner which is less harsh and less apt to promote strife. I am firmly persuaded that if schools throughout the world were under a single international authority, and if this authority devoted itself to clarifying the use of words calculated to promote passion, the existing hatreds between nations, creeds, and political parties would very rapidly diminish, and the preservation of peace throughout the world would become an easy matter. Meanwhile, those who stand for clear thinking and against mutual disastrous enmities have to work, not only against passions to which human nature is all too prone, but also against great organized forces of intolerance and insane self-assertion. In this struggle clear logical thinking, though only one of the actors, has a definite part to play.

History as an Art

I AM approaching the subject of this essay with considerable trepidation. I know that among my readers there are professional historians whom I greatly respect, and I should not at all wish to seem desirous of instructing them as to how their work should be done. I shall write as a consumer, not a producer. In shops they have a maxim: "The customer is always right." But academic persons (among whom I should wish to include myself) are more lordly than shopkeepers: if the consumer does not like what he is offered, that is because he is a Philistine and because he does not know what is good for him. Up to a point I sympathize with this attitude. It would never do for a mathematician to try to please the general reader. The physical sciences in their serious aspects must be addressed primarily to specialists, though their more adventurous practitioners write occasional books designed to make your flesh creep. But such books are not regarded by their fellow scientists as part of their serious work, and detract from, rather than add to, their professional reputation. I think that in this respect history is in a position different from that of mathematics and physical science. There have to be physicists, worse luck, and there have to be mathematicians until calculating machines become cheaper, but when that happy consummation has been reached, there will be no point in teaching anybody to do sums, and the multiplication table can be placed alongside the birch as an out-of-date instrument of education. But history seems to me to be in a different category. The multiplication table, though useful, can hardly be called beautiful. It is seldom that essential wisdom in regard to human destiny is to be found by remembering even its more difficult items. History, on the other hand, is—so I shall contend—a desirable part of everybody's mental furniture in the same kind of way as is generally recognized in the case of poetry. If history is to fulfill this function, it can only do so by appealing to those who are not professional historians. I have myself always found very great interest in the reading of history, and I have been grateful to those historians who gave me what I, as a consumer, though not a producer, was looking for in their books. It is from this point of view that I wish to write. I wish to set forth what those who are not historians ought to get from history. And this is a theme upon which you will, I think, admit that non-historians have a right to express an opinion.

There has been much argumentation, to my mind somewhat futile, as to whether history is a science or an art. It should, I think, have been entirely obvious that it is both. Trevelyan's *Social History of England* indubitably deserves praise from the artistic point of view, but I remember finding in it a statement to the effect that England's maritime greatness was due to a change in the habits of herrings. I know nothing about herrings, so I accept this statement on authority. My point is that it is a piece of science, and that its scientific character in no way detracts from the artistic value of Trevelyan's work. Nevertheless, the work of historians can be divided into two branches, according as the scientific or the artistic motive predominates.

When people speak of history as a science, there are two very different things that may be meant. There is a comparatively pedestrian sense in which science is involved in ascertaining historical facts. This is especially important in early history, where evidence is both scarce and obscure, but it arises also in more recent times whenever, as is apt to be the case, there is a conflict of testimony. How much are we to believe of Procopius? Is there anything of historical value to be made out of Napoleon's lucubrations in St. Helena? Such questions are in a sense scientific, since they concern the weight to be attached to different sources of evidence. They are matters as to which the historian may justifiably address himself to other historians, since the considerations involved are likely to be obscure and specialized. Work of this sort is presupposed in any attempt to write large-scale history. History, however much it may be pursued as an art, has to be controlled by the attempt to be true to fact. Truth to fact is a rule of the art, but does not in itself confer artistic excellence. It is like the rules of the sonnet, which can be scrupulously observed without conferring merit on the result. But history cannot be praiseworthy, even from the most purely artistic point of view, unless the historian does his utmost to preserve fidelity to the facts. Science in this sense is absolutely essential to the study of history.

There is another sense in which history attempts to be scientific, and this sense raises more difficult questions. In this sense history seeks to discover causal laws connecting different facts, in the same sort of way in which physical sciences have succeeded in discovering interconnections among facts. The attempt to discover such causal laws in history is entirely praiseworthy, but I do not think that it is what gives the most value to historical studies. I found an admirable discussion of this matter in an essay which I had read forty years ago and largely forgotten: I mean George Trevelyan's *Clio, a Muse*. He points out that in history we are interested in the particular facts and not only in their causal relations. It may be, as some have suggested, that Napoleon lost the Battle of Leipzig because he ate a peach after the Battle of Dresden. If this is the case, it is no doubt not without interest. But the events which it connects are on their own account much more interesting. In physical science, exactly the opposite is true. Eclipses, for example, are not very interesting in themselves except when they give fixed points in very early history, as is the case with the eclipse in Asia Minor which helps to date Thales and the eclipse in China in 776 B.C. (Some authorities say that it was in 775 B.C. I leave this question to historians and astronomers.) But although most eclipses are not interesting in themselves, the laws which determine their recurrence are of the very highest interest, and the discovery of these laws was of immense importance in dispelling superstition. Similarly, the experimental facts upon which modern physics is based would be totally uninteresting if it were not for the causal laws that they help to establish. But history is not like this. Most of the value of history is lost if we are not interested in the things that happen for their own sakes. In this respect history is like poetry. There is a satisfaction to curiosity in discovering why Coleridge wrote "Kubla Khan" as he did, but this satisfaction is a trivial affair compared to that which we derive from the poem itself.

I do not mean to deny that it is a good thing to discover causal sequences in history when it is possible, but I think the possibility exists only in rather limited fields. Gresham's law that bad money drives out good is an example of one of the best established of such causal sequences. The whole science of economics, in so far as it is valid, consists of causal laws illustrated by historical facts. But as everybody now recognizes, supposed laws of economics have a much more temporary and local validity than was thought a hundred years ago. One of the difficulties in searching for such laws is that there is not so much recurrence in history as in astronomy. It may be true, as Meyers maintains in his little book on *The*

Dawn of History, that on four separate occasions drought in Arabia has caused a wave of Semitic conquest, but it is hardly to be supposed that the same cause would produce the same effect at the present day. Even when historical causal sequences are established as regards the past, there is not much reason to expect that they will hold in the future, because the relevant facts are so complex that unforeseeable changes may falsify our predictions. No historian, however scientific, could have predicted in the fourteenth century the changes brought about by Columbus and Vasco da Gama. For these reasons I think that scientific laws in history are neither so important nor so discoverable as is sometimes maintained.

This applies with especial force to those large schemes of historical development which have fascinated many eminent men from St. Augustine to Professor Toynbee. In modern times, the most important inventors of general theories as to human development, have been Hegel and his disciple Marx. Both believed that the history of the past obeyed a logical schema, and that this same schema gave a means of foretelling the future. Neither foresaw the hydrogen bomb, and no doctrine of human development hitherto concocted enables us to foresee the effects of this ingenious device. If this reflection seems gloomy, I will add another of a more cheerful sort: I cannot accept the view of Spengler that every society must inevitably grow old and decay like an individual human body. I think this view results from unduly pressing the analogy between a social and an individual organism. Most societies have perished by assassination, and not by old age. Some might maintain that Chinese society has been decrepit ever since the fall of the Han dynasty; but it survived because the countries immediately to the west of China were sparsely inhabited. What has put an end to the traditional civilization of China is not any new inherent weakness, but the improve-

ment in means of communication with the West. Some among
the Stoics thought that the world would be periodically destroyed by fire and then recreated. There is evidently something in this view which suits men's preconceptions, and in
milder forms it underlies almost all general theories of human
development that historians have invented. All alike, I should
say, are no more than myths, agreeable or disagreeable according to the temperaments of their inventors.

There is a department of history which has always interested me, perhaps beyond its intrinsic importance. It is that
of bypaths in history: communities which have become isolated from the main current of their parent countries, but
have trickled by unforeseen courses into the main stream of
quite other rivers. From this point of view I have long been
fascinated by the Bactrian Greeks. I thought that they had
been completely lost, like a river absorbed by the desert, and
then I learned, to my no small delight, that they had become
the source of Buddhist art and had inspired the statuary of
the East through many ages and in many lands. Another example of the same kind of bypath is that of the Bogomils in
Bulgaria, who were obscure disciples of Marcian and Mani,
and whose doctrines, by means of certain misguided crusaders,
were adopted by the Cathari in northern Italy and the Albi-
genses in southern France. A still more remarkable example
of the same kind of thing appears in the history of New England. From early boyhood I had known of Pride's Purge,
when the haughty soldier caused the Long Parliament to
tremble in the name of theological truth and the wages due
to the army. But it had never occurred to me to wonder
what became of Pride after 1660. In 1896 I was taken to a
place in New England called Pride's Crossing, and was informed that it was called after the eponymous hero of the
Purge. I learned that he had had to leave his native country

and settle upon a wild and rocky shore where the winter was long, the soil infertile, and the Indians dangerous. It might have seemed to Charles II and his courtiers that Pride had met his deserts, but after two and a half centuries his descendants rule the world and the descendants of Charles II tremble at their frown.

I come now to my main theme, which is what history can do and should do for the general reader. I am not thinking of what history does for historians; I am thinking of history as an essential part of the furniture of an educated mind. We do not think that poetry should be read only by poets, or that music should be heard only by composers. And, in like manner, history should not be known only to historians. But clearly the kind of history which is to contribute to the mental life of those who are not historians must have certain qualities that more professional work need not have, and, conversely, does not require certain things which one would look for in a learned monograph. I will try to write—though I find it very difficult—what I feel that I personally have derived from the reading of history. I should put first and foremost something like a new dimension in the individual life, a sense of being a drop in a great river rather than a tightly bounded separate entity. The man whose interests are bounded by the short span between his birth and death has a myopic vision and a limitation of outlook which can hardly fail to narrow the scope of his hopes and desires. And what applies to an individual man, applies also to a community. Those communities that have as yet little history make upon a European a curious impression of thinness and isolation. They do not feel themselves the inheritors of the ages, and for that reason what they aim at transmitting to their successors seems jejune and emotionally poor to one in whom the past is vivid and the future is illuminated by knowledge of the slow and painful achievements of former times. History makes one aware that there is no finality in human affairs; there is not a static perfection and an unimprovable wisdom to be achieved. Whatever wisdom we may have achieved is a small matter in comparison with what is possible. Whatever beliefs we may cherish, even those that we deem most important, are not likely to last forever; and, if we imagine that they embody eternal verities, the future is likely to make a mock of us. Cocksure certainty is the source of much that is worst in our present world, and it is something of which the contemplation of history ought to cure us, not only or chiefly because there were wise men in the past, but because so much that was thought wisdom turned out to be folly—which suggests that much of our own supposed wisdom is no better.

I do not mean to maintain that we should lapse into a lazy skepticism. We should hold our beliefs, and hold them strongly. Nothing great is achieved without passion, but underneath the passion there should always be that large impersonal survey which sets limits to actions that our passions inspire. If you think ill of Communism or Capitalism, should you exterminate the human race in order that there may be no more Communists or Capitalists as the case may be? Few people would deliberately assert that this would be wise, and yet it is a consummation toward which some politicians who are not historically minded seem to be leading mankind. This is an extreme example, but it is by no means difficult to think of innumerable others.

Leaving these general and rather discursive considerations, let us come to the question how history should be written if it is to produce the best possible result in the nonhistorical reader. Here there is first of all an extremely simple requirement: it must be interesting. I mean that it must be interesting not only to men who for some special reason wish to know some set of historical facts, but to those who are reading in the same spirit in which one reads poetry or a good novel. This requires first and foremost that the historian should have feelings about the events that he is relating and the characters that he is portraying. It is of course imperative that the historian should not distort facts, but it is not imperative that he should not take sides in the clashes and conflicts that fill his pages. An historian who is impartial, in the sense of not liking one party better than another and not allowing himself to have heroes and villains among his characters, will be a dull writer. If the reader is to be interested, he must be allowed to take sides in the drama. If this causes an historian to be one-sided, the only remedy is to find another historian with an opposite bias. The history of the Reformation, for example, can be interesting when it is written by a Protestant historian, and can be equally interesting when it is written by a Catholic historian. If you wish to know what it felt like to live at the time of the Wars of Religion you will perhaps succeed if you read both Protestant and Catholic histories, but you will not succeed if you read only men who view the whole series of events with complete detachment. Carlyle said about his history of the French Revolution that his book was itself a kind of French Revolution. This is true, and it gives the book a certain abiding merit in spite of its inadequacy as an historical record. As you read it you understand why people did what they did, and this is one of the most important things that a history ought to do for the reader. At one time I read what Diodorus Siculus has to say about Agathocles, who appeared as an unmitigated ruffian. I looked up Agathocles afterward in a modern reference book and found him represented as bland and statesmanlike and probably innocent of all the crimes imputed to him. I have no means of knowing which

of these two accounts is the more true, but ....
whitewashing account was completely uninter.....
like a tendency, to which some modern historia...
to tone down everything dramatic and make ou....
were not so very heroic and villains not so very........
No doubt a love of drama can lead an historian a....y; but there is drama in plenty that requires no falsification, though only literary skill can convey it to the reader.

"Literary skill" is a large and general phrase, and it may be worth while to give it a more specific meaning. There is, first of all, style in the narrow sense of the word, especially diction and rhythm. Some words, especially those invented for scientific purposes, have merely a dictionary meaning. If you found the word "tetrahedron" on a page, you would at once begin to feel bored. But the word "pyramid" is a fine, rich word, which brings Pharaohs and Aztecs floating into the mind. Rhythm is a matter dependent upon emotion: What is strongly felt will express itself naturally in a rhythmical and varied form. For this reason, among others, a writer needs a certain freshness of feeling which is apt to be destroyed by fatigue and by the necessity of consulting authorities. I think—though this is perhaps counsel of perfection—that before an historian actually composes a chapter, he should have the material so familiarly in his mind that his pen never has to pause for verification of what he is saying. I do not mean that verification is unnecessary, because everybody's memory plays tricks, but that it should come after, and not during, composition. Style, when it is good, is a very personal expression of the writer's way of feeling, and for that reason, among others, it is fatal to imitate even the most admirable style. Somewhere in Milman's *History of Christianity* (I write from memory), he says: "Rhetoric was still studied as a fine, though considered as a mere, art." The shade of Gibbon, if it was looking over Milman's shoulder, must have been pained by this sentence.

If expository prose is to be interesting, there has to be a period of incubation, after the necessary knowledge has been acquired, when the bare facts will become clothed with such associations as are appropriate, of analogy or pathos or irony or what not, and when they will compose themselves into the unity of a pattern as in a play. This sort of thing is hardly likely to happen adequately unless the author has a fair amount of leisure and not an unfair amount of fatigue. Conscientious people are apt to work too hard and to spoil their work by doing so. Bagehot speaks somewhere of men he knew in the City who went bankrupt because they worked eight hours a day, but would have been rich if they had confined themselves to four hours. I think many learned men could profit by this analogy.

Within the compass of history as an art there are various kinds of history, each of which has its own peculiar kind of merit. One of these kinds of merit is especially exemplified by Gibbon, who offers us a stately procession of characters marching through the ages, all in court dress and yet all individual. Not long ago I was reading about Zenobia in the *Cambridge Ancient History*, but I regret to say that she appeared completely uninteresting. I remembered somewhat dimly a much more lively account in Gibbon. I looked it up, and at once the masterful lady came alive. Gibbon had had his feelings about her, and had imagined what it would be like to be at her court. He had written with lively fancy, and not merely with cold desire to chronicle known facts. It is odd that one does not more resent the fact that his characters all have to be fitted into an eighteenth-century mold. I remember that somewhere in dealing with the Vandals after the

time of Genseric he speaks of "the polished tyrants of Africa."
I am quite unable to believe that these men were polished,
though I have no difficulty in believing that they were tyrants.
But somehow, in spite of such limitations, Gibbon conveys an
extraordinarily vivid sense of the march of events throughout
the centuries with which he deals. His book illustrates what
I am firmly persuaded is true, that great history must be the
work of a single man and cannot possibly be achieved by a
compendium in which each contributor deals with his own
specialty. Learning has grown so multifarious and complex
that it has been thought impossible for any one mind to em-
brace a large field. I am sure that this is a most unfortunate
mistake. If a book is to have value except as a work of reference it must be the work of one mind. It must be the result of
holding together a great multiplicity within the unity of a
single temperament. I will admit at once that this is growing
more and more difficult, but I think means can be devised
by which it will still be possible, and I think they must be
devised if great histories are not to be a thing of the past.

What is needed is division of labor. Gibbon profited by
Tillemont, and probably could not otherwise have achieved
his work in a lifetime. The archaeologist or the man who
delves in unpublished manuscript material is likely to have
neither the time nor the energy for large-scale history. The
man who proposes to write large-scale history should not be
expected himself to do the spade work. In the sciences, this
sort of thing is recognized. Kepler's laws were based upon
the observations of Tycho Brahe. Clerk Maxwell's theories
rested upon the experiments of Faraday. Einstein did not himself make the observations upon which his doctrines are based.
Broadly speaking the amassing of facts is one thing, and the
digesting of them is another. Where the facts are numerous
and complex, it is scarcely possible for one man to do both.

Suppose, for example, you wish to know the effect of the Minoan civilization on the classical civilization of Greece. You will hardly expect the most balanced or the best informed opinion from a man who has been engaged in the very difficult work of ascertaining Minoan facts. The same sort of thing applies to less recondite problems, say, for example, the influence of Plutarch on the French Revolution.

The name of Plutarch brings to mind another department of history. History is not concerned only with large-scale pageants, nor with the delineation of different kinds of societies. It is concerned also, and equally, with individuals who are noteworthy on their own account. Plutarch's *Lives of the Noble Grecians and Romans* have inspired in many ambitious young men valiant careers upon which they might not otherwise have ventured. I think there is a tendency in our time to pay too little attention to the individual and too much to the mass. We are so persuaded that we live in the Age of the Common Man that men become common even when they might be otherwise. There has been a movement, especially in teaching history to the young, toward emphasis on types of culture as opposed to the doings of individual heroes. Up to a point, this is entirely praiseworthy. We get a better sense of the march of events if we are told something about the manner of life of Cromagnon man or Neanderthal man, and it is wholesome to know about the tenement houses in Rome where the Romans lived whom Plutarch does not mention. A book like the Hammonds' *Village Labourer* presents a whole period from a point of view of which there is nothing in the older conventional histories. All this is true and important. But what, though important, is not true, but most perniciously false, is the suggestion, which easily grows up when history is studied *only* in this way, that individuals do not count and that those who have been regarded as heroes are only embodiments of social forces, whose work would have been done by someone else if it had not been done by them, and that, broadly speaking, no individual can do better than let himself be borne along by the current of his time. What is worst about this view is that, if it is held, it tends to become true. Heroic lives are inspired by heroic ambitions, and the young man who thinks that there is nothing important to be done is pretty sure to do nothing important. For such reasons I think the kind of history that is exemplified by Plutarch's *Lives* is quite as necessary as the more generalized kind. Very few people can make a community: Lenin and Stalin are the only ones who have achieved it in modern times. But a very much larger number of men can achieve an individual life which is significant. This applies not only to men whom we may regard as models to be imitated, but to all those who afford new material for imagination. The Emperor Frederick II, for example, most certainly does not deserve to be imitated, but he makes a splendid piece in one's mental furniture. The Wonder of the World, tramping hither and thither with his menagerie, completed at last by his Prime Minister in a cage, debating with Moslem sages, winning crusades in spite of being excommunicate, is a figure that I should be sorry not to know about. We all think it worth while to know about the great heroes of tragedy—Agamemnon, Oedipus, Hamlet and the rest—but there have been real men whose lives had the same quality as that of the great tragic heroes, and had the additional merit of having actually existed. All forms of greatness, whether divine or diabolic, share a certain quality, and I do not wish to see this quality ironed out by the worship of mediocrity. When I first visited America nearly sixty years ago, I made the acquaintance of a lady who had lately had a son. Somebody remarked lightly, "perhaps he will be a genius." The lady, in tones of heartfelt horror, replied, "Oh, I hope not!" Her wish, alas, was granted.

I do not mean to subscribe to Carlyle's cult of heroes, still less to Nietzsche's exaggeration of it. I do not wish for one moment to suggest that the common man is unimportant, or that the study of masses of men is less worth pursuing than the study of notable individuals. I wish only to preserve a balance between the two. I believe that remarkable individuals have done a great deal to mold history. I think that, if the hundred ablest men of science of the seventeenth century had all died in infancy, the life of the common man in every industrial community would now be quite different from what it is. I do not think that if Shakespeare and Milton had not existed someone else would have composed their works. And yet this is the sort of thing that some "scientific" historians seem to wish one to believe.

I will go a step farther in agreement with those who emphasize the individual. I think that what is most worthy to be known and admired in human affairs has to do with individuals rather than with communities. I do not believe in the independent value of a collection of human beings over and above the value contained in their several lives, and I think it is dangerous if history neglects individual value in order to glorify a state, a nation, a church, or any other such collective entity. But I will not pursue this theme farther for fear of being led into politics.

The interest of the general reader in history has, I think, declined during the present century, and for my part I greatly regret this decline. There are a number of reasons for it. In the first place, reading altogether has declined. People go to the movies, or listen to the radio, or watch television. They indulge a curious passion for changing their position on the earth's surface as quickly as possible, which they combine with an attempt to make all parts of the earth's surface look alike. But even those who persist in the habit of serious reading spend less of their time on history than serious readers formerly did. My friend Whitehead at one time employed Paolo Sarpi's *History of the Council of Trent* as a bed book. I doubt whether there is now any person living who does likewise. History has ceased to be as interesting as it used to be, partly because the present is so full of important events, and so packed with quick-moving changes, that many people find neither time nor inclination to turn their attention to former centuries. A life of Hitler or Lenin or Stalin or Trotsky can be quite as interesting in itself as a life of Napoleon, and has, in addition, more relevance to present problems. But I am afraid we must admit that there is another cause for the decline of historical reading, and that is the decline of historical writing in the grand manner. I do not know how eagerly their contemporaries lapped up Herodotus or Thucydides or Polybius or Plutarch or Tacitus, but we all know the eagerness with which historians were welcomed in the eighteenth and nineteenth centuries. In Britain there was a long procession from Clarendon's *History of the Rebellion* to Macaulay. In France, from the time of Voltaire onward, history was a battleground of rival philosophies. In Germany, under the inspiration of Hegel, historians combined brilliance and wickedness in equal proportions. I do not think it would be unfair to Mommsen to say that his history had two themes: one, the greatness of Caesar because he destroyed liberty; the other, that Carthage was like England and Rome was like Germany and that the future Punic Wars to which he looked forward would have an outcome analogous to that of their predecessors. The influence of Treitschke in spreading a pernicious myth is generally recognized. When we speak of the importance of history, we must admit its importance for evil as well as for good. This applies especially to the popular myths which have gradually become a part of folklore. I went once to Ireland with my two young children. My daughter, aged five, made friends with a peasant woman who treated her with great kindness. But, as we went away, the woman said: "She's a bonny girl, in spite of Cromwell." It seemed a pity that the woman did not know either more history or less.

The decay in the writing of great histories is only part of the decay in the writing of great books. Men of science nowadays do not write books comparable to Newton's *Principia* or Darwin's *Origin of Species*. Poets no longer write epics. In the learned world, everything moves so fast that a massive book would be out of date before it could be published. Contributions to learning appear in periodicals, not in separate books, and few men in any branch of learning feel that there is time for that leisurely survey from which great books formerly sprang. There are of course exceptions. One of the most noteworthy is Professor Toynbee, whose work is as massive as any of those of former times. But the exceptions are not sufficiently numerous to disprove the general trend. I suppose the trend will remain until the world settles down to some form of progress less helter-skelter than the present race toward the abyss.

I think that in bringing sanity to our intoxicated age, history has an important part to play. I do not mean that this is to be brought about by any supposed "lessons of history," or indeed by anything easily put into a verbal formula. What history can and should do, not only for historians but for all whose education has given them any breadth of outlook, is to produce a certain temper of mind, a certain way of thinking and feeling about contemporary events and their relation to the past and the future. I do not know whether one should accept

Cornford's thesis that Thucydides modeled his history on Attic tragedy; but, if he did, the events that he recorded fully justified his doing so, and the Athenians, if they had seen themselves in the light of actors in a possible tragedy, might have had the wisdom to avert the tragic outcome. It is an ancient doctrine that tragedy comes of hubris, but it is none the less true for being ancient, and hubris recurs in every age among those who have forgotten the disasters to which it has always led. In our age, mankind collectively has given itself over to a degree of hubris surpassing everything known in former ages. In the past, Prometheus was regarded as a would-be liberator, restrained in his beneficent work by the tyranny of Zeus, but now we begin to wish that there were some Zeus to restrain the modern followers of Prometheus. Prometheus aimed to serve mankind: his modern followers serve the passions of mankind, but only in so far as they are mad and destructive. In the modern world there are clever men in laboratories and fools in power. The clever men are slaves, like Djinns in the *Arabian Nights*. Mankind collectively, under the guidance of the fools and by the ingenuity of the clever slaves, is engaged in the great task of preparing its own extermination. I wish there were a Thucydides to treat this theme as it deserves. I cannot but think that if the men in power were impregnated with a sense of history they would find a way of avoiding the catastrophe which all see approaching and which none desire, for history is not only an account of this nation or that, nor even of this continent or that; its theme is Man, that strange product of evolution which has risen by means of skill to a mastery over all other forms of life, and even, at great peril to himself, to mastery over the forces of inanimate nature. But Man, in spite of his cleverness, has not learned to think of the human family as one. Although he has abolished the jungle, he still allows himself to be governed by the law of the jungle. He has little sense of the common tasks of humanity, of its achievements in the past and its possible greater achievements in the future. He sees his fellow man not as a collaborator in a common purpose, but as an enemy who will kill if he is not killed. Whatever his sect or party may be, he believes that it embodies ultimate and eternal wisdom, and that the opposite party embodies ultimate and absolute folly. To any person with any historical culture such a view is absurd. No portion of mankind in the past was as good as it thought itself, or as bad as it was thought by its enemies; but, in the past, humanity could achieve its common purposes in spite of strife, though haltingly and with temporarily disastrous setbacks. But in our age the new cleverness is only compatible with survival if accompanied by a new wisdom. The wisdom that is needed is new only in one sense: that it must appeal to masses of men, and above all, to those who control great power. It is not new in the sense that it has never been proclaimed before. It has been proclaimed by wise men for many ages, but their wisdom has not been heeded. Now, the time is past when wisdom could be treated as nothing but the idle dream of visionaries. Sometimes in the moments when I am most oppressed by the fear of coming disaster, I am tempted to think that what the world needs is a Prophet who will proclaim, with a voice combining thunder with the deepest compassion, that the road upon which mankind is going is the wrong road—a road leading to the death of our children and to the extinction of all hope—but that there is another road which men can pursue if they will, and that this other road leads to a better world than any that has existed in the past. But, although this vision of a prophet can afford a momentary consolation, what the world needs is something more difficult, more rare. If a prophet were to arise in the East, he would be liquidated; if a prophet were to arise in the West, he would not be heard in the East and in the West would be condemned to obloquy. It is not by the action of any one individual, however great and however eloquent, that the world can be saved. It can be saved only when rulers and their followers in the most powerful countries of the world become aware that they have been pursuing a will-o'-the-wisp which is tempting them only toward ignominious death in a mire of futile hatred. The collective folly is not yet universal. Some nations stand wholly outside it, some are only partially victims to it. It is not too late to hope that mankind may have a future as well as a past. I believe that if men are to feel this hope with sufficient vividness to give it dynamic power, the awareness of history is one of the greatest forces of which the beneficent appeal must be felt.

How I Write

I CANNOT pretend to know how writing ought to be done, or what a wise critic would advise me to do with a view to improving my own writing. The most that I can do is to relate some things about my own attempts.

Until I was twenty-one, I wished to write more or less in the style of John Stuart Mill. I liked the structure of his sentences and his manner of developing a subject. I had, however, already a different ideal, derived, I suppose, from mathematics. I wished to say everything in the smallest number of words in which it could be said clearly. Perhaps, I thought, one should imitate Baedeker rather than any more literary model. I would spend hours trying to find the shortest way of saying something without ambiguity, and to this aim I was willing to sacrifice all attempts at aesthetic excellence.

At the age of twenty-one, however, I came under a new influence, that of my future brother-in-law, Logan Pearsall Smith. He was at that time exclusively interested in style as opposed to matter. His gods were Flaubert and Walter Pater, and I was quite ready to believe that the way to learn how to write was to copy their technique. He gave me various simple rules, of which I remember only two: "Put a comma every four words," and "never use 'and' except at the beginning of a sentence." His most emphatic advice was that one must always rewrite. I conscientiously tried this, but found that my first draft was almost always better than my second. This discovery has saved me an immense amount of time. I do not, of course, apply it to the substance, but only to the form. When I discover an error of an important kind, I rewrite the whole. What I do not find is that I can improve a sentence when I am satisfied with what it means.

Very gradually I have discovered ways of writing with a minimum of worry and anxiety. When I was young each fresh piece of serious work used to seem to me for a time—perhaps a long time—to be beyond my powers. I would fret myself into a nervous state from fear that it was never going to come right. I would make one unsatisfying attempt after another, and in the end have to discard them all. At last I found that such fumbling attempts were a waste of time. It appeared that after first contemplating a book on some subject, and after giving serious preliminary attention to it, I needed a period of subconscious incubation which could not be hurried and was if anything impeded by deliberate thinking. Sometimes I would find, after a time, that I had made a mistake, and that I could not write the book I had had in mind. But often I was more fortunate. Having, by a time of very intense concentration, planted the problem in my subconsciousness, it would germinate underground until, suddenly, the solution emerged with blinding clarity, so that it only remained to write down what had appeared as if in a revelation.

The most curious example of this process, and the one which led me subsequently to rely upon it, occurred at the beginning of 1914. I had undertaken to give the Lowell Lectures at Boston, and had chosen as my subject "Our Knowledge of the External World." Throughout 1913 I thought about this topic. In term time in my rooms at Cambridge, in vacations in a quiet inn on the upper reaches of the Thames, I concentrated with such intensity that I sometimes forgot to breathe and emerged panting as from a trance. But all to no avail. To every theory that I could think of I could perceive fatal objections. At last, in despair, I went off to Rome for Christmas, hoping that a holiday would revive my flagging energy. I got back to Cambridge on the last day of 1913, and although my difficulties were still completely unresolved I arranged, because the remaining time was short, to dictate as best as I could to a stenographer. Next morning, as she came in at the door, I suddenly saw exactly what I had to say, and proceeded to dictate the whole book without a moment's hesitation.

I do not want to convey an exaggerated impression. The book was very imperfect, and I now think that it contains serious errors. But it was the best that I could have done at that time, and a more leisurely method (within the time at my disposal) would almost certainly have produced something worse. Whatever may be true of other people, this is the right method for me. Flaubert and Pater, I have found, are best forgotten so far as I am concerned.

Although what I now think about how to write is not so very different from what I thought at the age of eighteen, my development has not been by any means rectilinear. There was a time, in the first years of this century, when I had more florid and rhetorical ambitions. This was the time when I wrote *A Free Man's Worship*, a work of which I do not now think well. At that time I was steeped in Milton's prose, and his rolling periods reverberated through the caverns of my mind. I cannot say that I no longer admire them, but for me to imitate them involves a certain insincerity. In fact, all imitation is dangerous. Nothing could be better in style than the Prayer Book and the Authorized Version of the Bible, but they express a way of thinking and feeling which is different from that of our time. A style is not good unless it is an intimate and almost involuntary expression of the personality of the writer, and then only if the writer's personality is worth expressing. But although direct imitation is always to be deprecated, there is much to be gained by familiarity with good prose, especially in cultivating a sense for prose rhythm.

There are some simple maxims—not perhaps quite so simple as those which my brother-in-law Logan Pearsall Smith offered me—which I think might be commended to writers of expository prose. First: never use a long word if a short word will do. Second: if you want to make a statement with a great many qualifications, put some of the qualifications in separate sentences. Third: do not let the beginning of your sentence lead the reader to an expectation which is contradicted by the end. Take, say, such a sentence as the following, which might occur in a work on sociology: "Human beings are completely exempt from undesirable behavior patterns only when certain prerequisites, not satisfied except in a small percentage of actual cases, have, through some fortuitous concourse of favorable circumstances, whether congenital or environmental, chanced to combine in producing an individual in whom many factors deviate from the norm in a socially advantageous manner." Let us see if we can translate this sentence into English. I suggest the following: "All men are scoundrels, or at any rate almost all. The men who are not must have had unusual luck, both in their birth and in their upbringing." This is shorter and more intelligible, and says just the same thing. But I am afraid any professor who used the second sentence instead of the first would get the sack.

This suggests a word of advice to such of my readers as may happen to be professors. I am allowed to use plain English because everybody knows that I could use mathematical logic if I chose. Take the statement: "Some people marry their deceased wives' sisters." I can express this in language which only becomes intelligible after years of study, and this gives me freedom. I suggest to young professors that their first work should be written in a jargon only to be understood by the erudite few. With that behind them, they can ever after say what they have to say in a language "understanded of the people." In these days, when our very lives are at the mercy of the professors, I cannot but think that they would deserve our gratitude if they adopted my advice.

The Road to Happiness

OR over two thousand years it has been the custom
among earnest moralists to decry happiness as something degraded and unworthy. The Stoics, for centuries, attacked Epicurus, who preached happiness; they said that
his was a pig's philosophy, and showed their superior virtue
by inventing scandalous lies about him. One of them, Clean-
thes, wanted Aristarchus persecuted for advocating the Co-
pernican system of astronomy; another, Marcus Aurelius,
persecuted the Christians; one of the most famous of them,
Seneca, abetted Nero's abominations, amassed a vast fortune,
and lent money to Boadicea at such an exorbitant rate of interest that she was driven into rebellion. So much for antiq
uity. Skipping the next 2,000 years, we come to the German
professors who invented the disastrous theories that led Germany to its downfall and the rest of the world to its present
perilous state; all these learned men despised happiness, as did
their British imitator, Carlyle, who is never weary of telling
us that we ought to eschew happiness in favor of blessedness.
He found blessedness in rather odd places: Cromwell's Irish
massacres, Frederick the Great's bloodthirsty perfidy, and
Governor Eyre's Jamaican brutality. In fact, contempt for
happiness is usually contempt for other people's happiness,
and is an elegant disguise for hatred of the human race. Even
when a man genuinely sacrifices his own happiness in favor of
something that he thinks nobler, he is apt to remain envious of
those who enjoy a lesser degree of nobility, and this envy
will, all too often, make those who think themselves saints

cruel and destructive. In our day the most important examples of this mentality are the Communists.

People who have theories as to how one should live tend to forget the limitations of nature. If your way of life involves constant restraint of impulse for the sake of some one supreme aim that you have set yourself, it is likely that the aim will become increasingly distasteful because of the efforts that it demands; impulse, denied its normal outlets, will find others, probably in spite; pleasure, if you allow yourself any at all, will be dissociated from the main current of your life, and will become Bacchic and frivolous. Such pleasure brings no happiness, but only a deeper despair.

It is a commonplace among moralists that you cannot get happiness by pursuing it. This is only true if you pursue it unwisely. Gamblers at Monte Carlo are pursuing money, and most of them lose it instead, but there are other ways of pursuing money which often succeed. So it is with happiness. If you pursue it by means of drink, you are forgetting the hangover. Epicurus pursued it by living in congenial society and eating only dry bread, supplemented by a little cheese on feast days. His method proved successful, in his case, but he was a valetudinarian, and most people would need something more vigorous. For most people, the pursuit of happiness, unless supplemented in various ways, is too abstract and theoretical to be adequate as a personal rule of life. But I think that whatever personal rule of life you may choose, it should not, except in rare heroic cases, be incompatible with happiness.

There are a great many people who have the material conditions of happiness, i.e. health and a sufficient income, and who, nevertheless, are profoundly unhappy. This is especially true in America. In such cases it would seem as if the fault must lie with a wrong theory as to how to live. In one sense we may say that any theory as to how to live is wrong.

We imagine ourselves more different from the animals than
we are. Animals live on impulse, and are happy as long as external conditions are favorable. If you have a cat, it will enjoy life if it has food and warmth and opportunities for an
occasional night on the tiles. Your needs are more complex
than those of your cat, but they still have their basis in instinct. In civilized societies, especially in English-speaking societies, this is too apt to be forgotten. People propose to themselves some one paramount objective, and restrain all impulses
that do not minister to it. A businessman may be so anxious
to grow rich that to this end he sacrifices health and the private affections. When at last he has become rich, no pleasure
remains to him except harrying other people by exhortations
to imitate his noble example. Many rich ladies, although nature has not endowed them with any spontaneous pleasure in
literature or art, decide to be thought cultured, and spend
boring hours learning the right thing to say about fashionable
new books. It does not occur to them that books are written
to give delight, not to afford opportunities for a dusty snob-
bism.

If you look about you at the men and women whom you
can call happy, you will see that they all have certain things in
common. The most important of these things is an activity
which at most times is enjoyable on its own account, and
which, in addition, gradually builds up something that you
are glad to see coming into existence. Women who take an
instinctive pleasure in their children (which many women,
especially educated women, do not) can get this kind of satisfaction out of bringing up a family. Artists and authors and
men of science get happiness in this way if their own work
seems good to them. But there are many humbler forms of
the same kind of pleasure. Many men who spend their working life in the City devote their weekends to voluntary and

unremunerated toil in their gardens, and when the spring comes they experience all the joys of having created beauty.

It is impossible to be happy without activity, but it is also impossible to be happy if the activity is excessive or of a repulsive kind. Activity is agreeable when it is directed very obviously to a desired end and is not in itself contrary to impulse. A dog will pursue rabbits to the point of complete exhaustion and be happy all the time, but if you put the dog on a treadmill and gave him a good dinner after half an hour, he would not be happy till he got the dinner, because he would not have been engaged in a natural activity meanwhile. One of the difficulties of our time is that, in a complex modern society, few of the things that have to be done have the naturalness of hunting. The consequence is that most people, in a technically advanced community, have to find their happiness outside the work by which they make their living. And if their work is exhausting their pleasures will tend to be passive. Watching a football match or going to the cinema leaves little satisfaction afterward, and does not in any degree gratify creative impulses. The satisfaction of the players, who are active, is of quite a different order.

The wish to be respected by neighbors and the fear of being despised by them drive men and women (especially women) into ways of behavior which are not prompted by any spontaneous impulse. The person who is always "correct" is always bored, or almost always. It is heartrending to watch mothers teaching their children to curb their joy of life and become sedate puppets, lest they should be thought to belong to a lower social class than that to which their parents aspire.

The pursuit of social success, in the form of prestige or power or both, is the most important obstacle to happiness in a competitive society. I am not denying that success is an ingredient in happiness—to some, a very important ingredient.

But it does not, by itself, suffice to satisfy most people. You may be rich and admired, but if you have no friends, no interests, no spontaneous useless pleasures, you will be miserable. Living for social success is one form of living by a theory, and all living by theory is dusty and desiccating.

If a man or woman who is healthy and has enough to eat is to be happy, there is need of two things that, at first sight, might seem antagonistic. There is need, first, of a stable framework built round a central purpose, and second, of what may be called "play," that is to say, of things that are done merely because they are fun, and not because they serve some serious end. The settled framework must be an embodiment of fairly constant impulses, e.g. those connected with family or work. If the family has become steadily hateful, or the work uniformly irksome, they can no longer bring happiness; but it is worth while to endure occasional hatefulness or irksomeness if they are not felt continually. And they are much less likely to be felt continually if advantage is taken of opportunities for "play."

The whole subject of happiness has, in my opinion, been treated too solemnly. It has been thought that men cannot be happy without a theory of life or a religion. Perhaps those who have been rendered unhappy by a bad theory may need a better theory to help them to recovery, just as you may need a tonic when you have been ill. But when things are normal a man should be healthy without a tonic and happy without a theory. It is the simple things that really matter. If a man delights in his wife and children, has success in work, and finds pleasure in the alternation of day and night, spring and autumn, he will be happy whatever his philosophy may be. If, on the other hand, he finds his wife hateful, his children's noise unendurable, and the office a nightmare; if in the daytime he longs for night, and at night he sighs for the light of day—then what he needs is not a new philosophy but a new regimen—a different diet, or more exercise, or what not. Man is an animal, and his happiness depends upon his physiology more than he likes to think. This is a humble conclusion, but I cannot make myself disbelieve it. Unhappy businessmen, I am convinced, would increase their happiness more by walking six miles every day than by any conceivable change of philosophy. This, incidentally, was the opinion of Jefferson, who on this ground deplored the horse. Language would have failed him if he could have foreseen the motor car.

Symptoms of Orwell's *1984*

G EORGE ORWELL'S *1984* is a gruesome book which duly made its readers shudder. It did not, however, have the effect which no doubt its author intended. People remarked that Orwell was very ill when he wrote it, and in fact died soon afterward. They rather enjoyed the *frisson* that its horrors gave them and thought: "Oh well, of course it will never be as bad as that except in Russia! Obviously the author enjoys gloom; and so do we, as long as we don't take it seriously." Having soothed themselves with these comfortable falsehoods, people proceeded on their way to make Orwell's prognostications come true. Bit by bit, and step by step, the world has been marching toward the realization of Orwell's nightmares; but because the march has been gradual, people have not realized how far it has taken them on this fatal road.

Only those who remember the world before 1914 can adequately realize how much has already been lost. In that happy age, one could travel without a passport, everywhere except in Russia. One could freely express any political opinion, except in Russia. Press censorship was unknown, except in Russia. Any white man could emigrate freely to any part of the world. The limitations of freedom in Czarist Russia were regarded with horror throughout the rest of the civilized world, and the power of the Russian Secret Police was regarded as an abomination. Russia is still worse than the Western World, not because the Western World has preserved its liberties, but because, while it has been losing them, Russia has marched farther in the direction of tyranny than any Czar ever thought of going.

For a long time after the Russian Revolution, it was customary to say, "No doubt the new regime has its faults, but at any rate it is better than that which it has superseded." This was a complete delusion. When one rereads accounts of exile in Siberia under the Czar, it is impossible to recapture the revulsion with which one read them long ago. The exiles had a very considerable degree of liberty, both mental and physical, and their lot was in no way comparable to that of people subjected to forced labor under the Soviet Government. Educated Russians could travel freely and enjoy contacts with Western Europeans which are now impossible. Opposition to the Government, although it was apt to be punished, was possible, and the punishment as a rule was nothing like as severe as it has become. Nor did tyranny extend nearly as widely as it does now. I read recently the early life of Trotsky as related by Deutscher, and it reveals a degree of political and intellectual freedom to which there is nothing comparable in present-day Russia. There is still as great a gulf between Russia and the West as there was in Czarist days, but I do not think the gulf is greater than it was then, for, while Russia has grown worse, the West also has lost much of the freedom which it formerly enjoyed.

The problem is not new except quantitatively. Ever since civilization began, the authorities of most States have persecuted the best men among their subjects. We are all shocked by the treatment of Socrates and Christ, but most people do not realize that such has been the fate of a large proportion of the men subsequently regarded as unusually admirable. Most of the early Greek philosophers were refugees. Aristotle was protected from the hostility of Athens only by Alexander's armies, and, when Alexander died, Aristotle had to fly. In the seventeenth century scientific innovators were persecuted almost everywhere except in Holland. Spinoza would have had no chance to do his work if he had not been Dutch. Descartes and Locke found it prudent to flee to Holland. When England, in 1688, acquired a Dutch king, it took over Dutch tolerance and has been, ever since, more liberal than most states, except during the period of the wars against revolutionary France and Napoleon. In most countries at most times, whatever subsequently came to be thought best was viewed with horror at the time by those who wielded authority.

What is new in our time is the increased power of the authorities to enforce their prejudices. The police everywhere are very much more powerful than at any earlier time; and the police, while they serve a purpose in suppressing ordinary crime, are apt to be just as active in suppressing extraordinary merit.

The problem is not confined to this country or that, although the intensity of the evil is not evenly distributed. In my own country things are done more quietly and with less fuss than in the United States, and the public knows very much less about them. There have been purges of the Civil Service carried out without any of the business of Congressional Committees. The Home Office, which controls immigration, is profoundly illiberal except when public opinion can be mobilized against it. A Polish friend of mine, a very brilliant writer who had never been a Communist, applied for naturalization in England after living in that country for a long time, but his request was at first refused on the ground that he was a friend of the Polish Ambassador. His request was only granted in the end as a result of protests by various people of irreproachable reputation. The right of asylum for political refugees that used to be England's boast has now been abandoned by the Home Office, though perhaps it may be restored as the result of agitation.

There is a reason for the general deterioration as regards liberty. This reason is the increased power of organizations and the increasing degree to which men's actions are controlled by this or that large body. In every organization there are two purposes: one, the ostensible purpose for which the organization exists; the other, the increase in the power of its officials. This second purpose is very likely to make a stronger appeal to the officials concerned than the general public purpose that they are expected to serve. If you fall foul of the police by attempting to expose some iniquity of which they have been guilty, you may expect to incur their hostility; and, if so, you are very likely to suffer severely.

I have found among many liberal-minded people a belief that all is well so long as the law courts decide rightly when a case comes before them. This is entirely unrealistic. Suppose, for example, to take a by no means hypothetical case, that a professor is dismissed on a false charge of disloyalty. He may, if he happens to have rich friends, be able to establish in court that the charge was false, but this will probably take years during which he will starve or depend on charity. At the end he is a marked man. The university authorities, having learned wisdom, will say that he is a bad lecturer and does insufficient research. He will find himself again dismissed, this time without redress and with little hope of employment elsewhere.

There are, it is true, some educational institutions in America which, so far, have been strong enough to hold out. This, however, is only possible for an institution which has great prestige and has brave men in charge of its policy. Consider, for example, what Senator McCarthy has said about Harvard. He said he "couldn't conceive of anyone sending children to

Harvard University where they would be open to indoctrination by Communist professors." At Harvard, he said, there is a "smelly mess which people sending sons and daughters there should know about." Institutions less eminent than Harvard could hardly face such a blast.

The power of the police, however, is a more serious and a more universal phenomenon than Senator McCarthy. It is, of course, greatly increased by the atmosphere of fear which exists on both sides of the Iron Curtain. If you live in Russia and cease to be sympathetic with Communism, you will suffer unless you keep silence even in the bosom of your family. In America, if you have been a Communist and you cease to be, you are also liable to penalties, not legal—unless you have been trapped into perjury—but economic and social. There is only one thing that you can do to escape such penalties, and that is to sell yourself to the Department of Justice as an informer, when your success will depend upon what tall stories you can get the FBI to believe.

The increase of organization in the modern world demands new institutions if anything in the way of liberty is to be preserved. The situation is analogous to that which arose through the increased power of monarchs in the sixteenth century. It was against their excessive power that the whole fight of traditional liberalism was fought and won. But after their power had faded, new powers at least as dangerous arose, and the worst of these in our day is the power of the police. There is, so far as I can see, only one possible remedy, and that is the establishment of a second police force designed to prove innocence, not guilt. People often say that it is better that ninety-nine guilty men should escape than that one innocent man should be punished. Our institutions are founded upon the opposite view. If a man is accused, for example, of a murder, all the resources of the State, in the shape of policemen and detectives, are employed to prove his guilt, whereas it is left to his individual efforts to prove his innocence. If he employs detectives, they have to be private detectives paid out of his own pocket or that of his friends. Whatever his employment may have been, he will have neither time nor opportunity to continue earning money by means of it. The lawyers for the prosecution are paid by the State. His lawyers have to be paid by him, unless he pleads poverty, and then they will probably be less eminent than those of the prosecution. All this is quite unjust. It is at least as much in the public interest to prove that an innocent man has not committed a crime, as it is to prove that a guilty man has committed it. A police force designed to prove innocence should never attempt to prove guilt except in one kind of case: namely, where it is the authorities who are suspected of a crime. I think that the creation of such a second police force might enable us to preserve some of our traditional liberties, but I do not think that any lesser measure will do so.

One of the worst things resulting from the modern increase of the powers of the authorities is the suppression of truth and the spread of falsehood by means of public agencies. Russians are kept as far as possible in ignorance about Western countries, to the degree that people in Moscow imagine theirs to be the only subway in the world. Chinese intellectuals, since China became Communist, have been subjected to a horrible process called "brain-washing." Learned men who have acquired all the knowledge to be obtained in their subject from America or Western Europe are compelled to abjure what they have learned and to state that everything worth knowing is to be derived from Communist sources. They are subjected to such psychological pressure that they emerge broken men, able only to repeat, parrot fashion, the jejune formulas handed down by their official superiors. In

Russia and China this sort of thing is enforced by direct penalties, not only to recalcitrant individuals, but also to their families. In other countries the process has not yet gone so far. Those who reported truthfully about the evils of Chiang Kai-shek's regime during the last years of his rule in China were not liquidated, but everything possible was done to prevent their truthful reports from being believed, and they became suspects in degrees which varied according to their eminence. A man who reports truly to his government about what he finds in a foreign country, unless his report agrees with official prejudices, not only runs a grave personal risk, but knows that his information will be ignored. There is, of course, nothing new in this except in degree. In 1899, General Butler, who was in command of British forces in South Africa, reported that it would require an army of at least two hundred thousand to subdue the Boers. For this unpopular opinion he was demoted, and was given no credit when the opinion turned out to be correct. But, although the evil is not new, it is very much greater in extent than it used to be. There is no longer, even among those who think themselves more or less liberal, a belief that it is a good thing to study all sides of a question. The purging of United States libraries in Europe and of school libraries in America, is designed to prevent people from knowing more than one side of a question. The *Index Expurgatorius* has become a recognized part of the policy of those who say that they fight for freedom. Apparently the authorities no longer have sufficient belief in the justice of their cause to think that it can survive the ordeal of free discussion. Only so long as the other side is unheard are they confident of obtaining credence. This shows a sad decay in the robustness of our belief in our own institutions. During the war, the Nazis did not permit Germans to listen to British radio, but nobody in England was hindered from listen-

ing to the German radio because our faith in our own cause
was unshakable. So long as we prevent Communists from being heard, we produce the impression that they must have a
very strong case. Free speech used to be advocated on the
ground that free discussion would lead to the victory of the
better opinion. This belief is being lost under the influence of
fear. The result is that truth is one thing and "official truth"
is another. This is the first step on the road to Orwell's "dou-
ble-talk" and "double-think." It will be said that the legal existence of free speech has been preserved, but its effective existence is disastrously curtailed if the more important means
of publicity are only open to opinions which have the sanc-
tion of orthodoxy.

This applies more particularly to education. Even mildly
liberal opinions expose an educator nowadays in some important countries to the risk of losing his job and being unable to
find any other. The consequence is that children grow up in
ignorance of many things that it is vitally important they
should know, and that bigotry and obscurantism have a perilous measure of popular support.

Fear is the source from which all these evils spring, and
fear, as is apt to happen in a panic, inspires the very actions
which bring about the disasters that are dreaded. The dangers are real—they are indeed greater than at any previous
time in human history—but all yielding to hysteria increases
them. It is our clear duty in this difficult time, not only to
know the dangers, but to view them calmly and rationally in
spite of knowledge of their magnitude. Orwell's world of
1984, if we allow it to exist, will not exist for long. It will be
only the prelude to universal death.

Why I Am Not a Communist*

I**N RELATION** to any political doctrine there are two questions to be asked: (1) Are its theoretical tenets true? (2) Is its practical policy likely to increase human happiness? For my part, I think the theoretical tenets of Communism are false, and I think its practical maxims are such as to produce an immeasurable increase of human misery.

The theoretical doctrines of Communism are for the most part derived from Marx. My objections to Marx are of two sorts: one, that he was muddleheaded; and the other, that his thinking was almost entirely inspired by hatred. The doctrine of surplus value, which is supposed to demonstrate the exploitation of wage-earners under Capitalism, is arrived at: (a) by surreptitiously accepting Malthus' doctrine of population, which Marx and all his disciples explicitly repudiate; (b) by applying Ricardo's theory of value to wages, but not to the prices of manufactured articles. He is entirely satisfied with the result, not because it is in accordance with the facts or because it is logically coherent, but because it is calculated to rouse fury in wage-earners. Marx's doctrine that all historical events have been motivated by class conflicts is a rash and untrue extension to world history of certain features prominent in England and France a hundred years ago. His belief that there is a cosmic force called Dialectical Materialism which governs human history independently of human volitions, is mere mythology. His theoretical errors, however,

* Originally appeared in the Background Book, *Why I Opposed Communism*, published by Phoenix House, Ltd.

would not have mattered so much but for the fact that, like Tertullian and Carlyle, his chief desire was to see his enemies punished, and he cared little what happened to his friends in the process.

Marx's doctrine was bad enough, but the developments which it underwent under Lenin and Stalin made it much worse. Marx had taught that there would be a revolutionary transitional period following the victory of the Proletariat in a civil war and that during this period the Proletariat, in accordance with the usual practice after a civil war, would deprive its vanquished enemies of political power. This period was to be that of the dictatorship of the Proletariat. It should not be forgotten that in Marx's prophetic vision the victory of the Proletariat was to come after it had grown to be the vast majority of the population. The dictatorship of the Proletariat therefore as conceived by Marx was not essentially antidemocratic. In the Russia of 1917, however, the Proletariat was a small percentage of the population, the great majority being peasants. It was decreed that the Bolshevik party was the class-conscious part of the Proletariat, and that a small committee of its leaders was the class-conscious part of the Bolshevik party. The dictatorship of the Proletariat thus came to be the dictatorship of a small committee, and ultimately of one man—Stalin. As the sole class-conscious Proletarian, Stalin condemned millions of peasants to death by starvation and millions of others to forced labor in concentration camps. He even went so far as to decree that the laws of heredity are henceforth to be different from what they used to be, and that the germ plasm is to obey Soviet decrees but not that reactionary priest Mendel. I am completely at a loss to understand how it came about that some people who are both humane and intelligent could find something to admire in the vast slave camp produced by Stalin.

I have always disagreed with Marx. My first hostile criticism of him was published in 1896. But my objections to modern Communism go deeper than my objections to Marx. It is the abandonment of democracy that I find particularly disastrous. A minority resting its power upon the activities of a secret police is bound to be cruel, oppressive and obscurantist. The dangers of irresponsible power came to be generally recognized during the eighteenth and nineteenth centuries, but those who have been dazzled by the outward success of the Soviet Union have forgotten all that was painfully learned during the days of absolute monarchy, and have gone back to what was worst in the Middle Ages under the curious delusion that they were in the vanguard of progress.

There are signs that in course of time the Russian regime will become more liberal. But, although this is possible, it is very far from certain. In the meantime, all those who value not only art and science but a sufficiency of daily bread and freedom from the fear that a careless word by their children to a schoolteacher may condemn them to forced labor in a Siberian wilderness, must do what lies in their power to preserve in their own countries a less servile and more prosperous manner of life.

There are those who, oppressed by the evils of Communism, are led to the conclusion that the only effective way to combat these evils is by means of a world war. I think this a mistake. At one time such a policy might have been possible, but now war has become so terrible and Communism has become so powerful that no one can tell what would be left after a world war, and whatever might be left would probably be at least as bad as present-day Communism. This forecast does not depend upon which side, if either, is nominally victorious. It depends only upon the inevitable effects of mass destruction by means of hydrogen and cobalt bombs and per-

haps of ingeniously propagated plagues. The way to combat
Communism is not war. What is needed in addition to such
armaments as will deter Communists from attacking the
West, is a diminution of the grounds for discontent in the
less prosperous parts of the non-Communist world. In most
of the countries of Asia, there is abject poverty which the
West ought to alleviate as far as it lies in its power to do so.
There is also a great bitterness which was caused by the
centuries of European insolent domination in Asia. This
ought to be dealt with by a combination of patient tact with
dramatic announcements renouncing such relics of white
domination as survive in Asia. Communism is a doctrine bred
of poverty, hatred and strife. Its spread can only be arrested
by diminishing the area of poverty and hatred.

Man's Peril

I AM writing on this occasion not as a Briton, not as a European, not as a member of a Western democracy, but as a human being, a member of the species Man, whose continued existence is in doubt. The world is full of conflicts: Jews and Arabs; Indians and Pakistanis; white men and Negroes in Africa; and, overshadowing all minor conflicts, the titanic struggle between Communism and anti-Communism.

Almost everybody who is politically conscious has strong feelings about one or more of these issues; but I want you, if you can, to set aside such feelings for the moment and consider yourself only as a member of a biological species which has had a remarkable history and whose disappearance none of us can desire. I shall try to write no single word which should appeal to one group rather than to another. All, equally, are in peril, and, if the peril is understood, there is hope that they may collectively avert it. We have to learn to think in a new way. We have to learn to ask ourselves not what steps can be taken to give military victory to whatever group we prefer, for there no longer are such steps. The question we have to ask ourselves is: What steps can be taken to prevent a military contest of which the issue must be disastrous to all sides?

The general public, and even many men in positions of authority, have not realized what would be involved in a war with hydrogen bombs. The general public still thinks in terms of the obliteration of cities. It is understood that the new bombs are more powerful than the old and that, while one atomic bomb could obliterate Hiroshima, one hydrogen bomb could obliterate the largest cities such as London, New York, and Moscow. No doubt in a hydrogen-bomb war great cities would be obliterated. But this is one of the minor disasters that would have to be faced. If everybody in London, New York, and Moscow were exterminated, the world might, in the course of a few centuries, recover from the blow. But we now know, especially since the Bikini test, that hydrogen bombs can gradually spread destruction over a much wider area than had been supposed. It is stated on very good authority that a bomb can now be manufactured which will be 25,000 times as powerful as that which destroyed Hiroshima. Such a bomb, if exploded near the ground or underwater, sends radioactive particles into the upper air. They sink gradually and reach the surface of the earth in the form of a deadly dust or rain. It was this dust which infected the Japanese fishermen and their catch of fish although they were outside what American experts believed to be the danger zone. No one knows how widely such lethal radioactive particles might be diffused, but the best authorities are unanimous in saying that a war with hydrogen bombs is quite likely to put an end to the human race. It is feared that if many hydrogen bombs are used there will be universal death—sudden only for a fortunate minority, but for the majority a slow torture of disease and disintegration.

I will give a few instances out of many. Sir John Slessor, who can speak with unrivaled authority from his experiences of air warfare, has said: "A world war in this day and age would be general suicide"; and has gone on to state: "It never has and never will make any sense trying to abolish any particular *weapon* of war. What we have got to abolish is *war*." Lord Adrian, who is the leading English authority on nerve physiology, recently emphasized the same point in his address as president of the British Association. He said: "We must face the possibility that repeated atomic explosions will lead to a degree of general radioactivity which no one can tolerate or escape"; and he added: "Unless we are ready to give up some of our old loyalties, we may be forced into a fight which might end the human race." Air Chief Marshal Sir Philip Joubert says: "With the advent of the hydrogen bomb, it would appear that the human race has arrived at a point where it must abandon war as a continuation of policy or accept the possibility of total destruction." I could prolong such quotations indefinitely.

Many warnings have been uttered by eminent men of science and by authorities in military strategy. None of them will say that the worst results are certain. What they do say is that these results are possible and no one can be sure that they will not be realized. I have not found that the views of experts on this question depend in any degree upon their politics or prejudices. They depend only, so far as my researches have revealed, upon the extent of the particular expert's knowledge. I have found that the men who know most are most gloomy.

Stark, Inescapable Problem

Here, then, is the problem which I present to you, stark and dreadful and inescapable: Shall we put an end to the human race; or shall mankind renounce war? People will not face this alternative because it is so difficult to abolish war. The abolition of war will demand distasteful limitations of national sovereignty. But what perhaps impedes understanding of the situation more than anything else is that the term "mankind" feels vague and abstract. People scarcely realize in imagination that the danger is to themselves and their children and their grandchildren, and not only to a dimly apprehended humanity. And so they hope that perhaps war may be allowed to continue provided modern weapons are prohibited. I am afraid this hope is illusory. Whatever agreements not to use hydrogen bombs had been reached in time of peace, they would no longer be considered binding in time of war, and both sides would set to work to manufacture hydrogen bombs as soon as war broke out, for if one side manufactured the bombs and the other did not, the side that manufactured them would inevitably be victorious.

On both sides of the Iron Curtain there are political obstacles to emphasis on the destructive character of future war. If either side were to announce that it would on no account resort to war, it would be diplomatically at the mercy of the other side. Each side, for the sake of self-preservation, must continue to say that there are provocations that it will not endure. Each side may long for an accommodation, but neither side dare express this longing convincingly. The position is analogous to that of duelists in former times. No doubt it frequently happened that each of the duelists feared death and desired an accommodation, but neither could say so, since, if he did, he would be thought a coward. The only hope in such cases was intervention by friends of both parties suggesting an accommodation to which both could agree at the same moment. This is an exact analogy to the present position of the protagonists on either side of the Iron Curtain. If an agreement making war improbable is to be reached, it will have to be by the friendly offices of neutrals, who can speak of the disastrousness of war without being accused of advocating a policy of "appeasement." The neutrals have every right, even from the narrowest consideration of self-interest, to do whatever lies in their power to prevent the outbreak of a world war, for if such a war does break out, it is highly probable that all the inhabitants of neutral countries, along

with the rest of mankind, will perish. If I were in control of a
neutral government, I should certainly consider it my paramount duty to see to it that my country would continue to
have inhabitants, and the only way by which I could make
this probable would be to promote some kind of accommodation between the powers on opposite sides of the Iron Curtain.

I, personally, am of course not neutral in my feeling and I
should not wish to see the danger of war averted by an abject submission of the West. But, as a human being, I have to
remember that, if the issues between East and West are to be
decided in any manner that can give any possible satisfaction
to anybody, whether Communist or anti-Communist, whether
Asian or European or American, whether white or black,
then these issues must not be decided by war. I should
wish this to be understood on both sides of the Iron Curtain.
It is emphatically not enough to have it understood on one
side only. I think the neutrals, since they are not caught in
our tragic dilemma, can, if they will, bring about this realization on both sides. I should like to see one or more neutral
powers appoint a commission of experts, who should all be
neutrals, to draw up a report on the destructive effects to be
expected in a war with hydrogen bombs, not only among the
belligerents but also among neutrals. I should wish this report
presented to the governments of all the Great Powers with
an invitation to express their agreement or disagreement
with its findings. I think it possible that in this way all the
Great Powers could be led to agree that a world war can no
longer serve the purposes of any of them, since it is likely to
exterminate friend and foe equally and neutrals likewise.

As geological time is reckoned, Man has so far existed only
for a very short period—1,000,000 years at the most. What
he has achieved, especially during the last 6,000 years, is

something utterly new in the history of the Cosmos, so far at least as we are acquainted with it. For countless ages the sun rose and set, the moon waxed and waned, the stars shone in the night, but it was only with the coming of Man that these things were understood. In the great world of astronomy and in the little world of the atom, Man has unveiled secrets which might have been thought undiscoverable. In art and literature and religion, some men have shown a sublimity of feeling which makes the species worth preserving. Is all this to end in trivial horror because so few are able to think of Man rather than of this or that group of men? Is our race so destitute of wisdom, so incapable of impartial love, so blind even to the simplest dictates of self-preservation, that the last proof of its silly cleverness is to be the extermination of all life on our planet?—for it will be not only men who will perish, but also the animals, whom no one can accuse of Communism or anti-Communism.

I cannot believe that this is to be the end. I would have men forget their quarrels for a moment and reflect that, if they will allow themselves to survive, there is every reason to expect the triumphs of the future to exceed immeasurably the triumphs of the past. There lies before us, if we choose, continual progress in happiness, knowledge, and wisdom. Shall we, instead, choose death, because we cannot forget our quarrels? I appeal, as a human being to human beings: remember your humanity, and forget the rest. If you can do so, the way lies open to a new Paradise; if you cannot, nothing lies before you but universal death.

Steps Toward Peace

*A speech by Bertrand Russell
delivered in his absence at the
World Assembly for Peace, Helsinki*

I SHOULD like to convey to this Assembly my regret that I cannot be present, and my hopes for a fruitful outcome.

Mankind is faced with an alternative which has never before arisen in human history: either war must be renounced or we must expect the annihilation of the human race. Many warnings have been uttered by eminent men of science and by authorities in military strategy. None of them will say that the worst results are certain.

What I think may be taken as certain, is that already there is no possibility of victory for either side as victory has been hitherto understood, and if scientific warfare continues unrestricted the next war would pretty certainly leave no survivors. It follows that the only possibilities before mankind are: peace by agreement or the peace of universal death.

The series of steps which I am suggesting will help us, I believe, to reach the happier alternative. There are, no doubt, other ways of attaining the same goal, but it is important if apathetic despair is not to paralyze our activities to have in mind at least one definite method of arriving at secure peace.

Before considering these steps, I should like to comment on a point of view advanced, as I think mistakenly, by genuine friends of peace who say that we need an agreement between the Powers never to use nuclear weapons. I believe the attempt to secure such an agreement to be a blind alley for two reasons. One of these is that such weapons can now be manufactured with a degree of secrecy that defies inspection. It follows that, even if an agreement prohibiting such weapons had been concluded, each side would think that the other was secretly making them and mutual suspicion would make relations even more strained than they are now.

The other argument is that, even if each side refrained from manufacturing such weapons while nominal peace lasted, neither side would feel bound by the agreement if war had actually broken out, and each side could manufacture many H-bombs after the fighting had begun.

There are many people who flatter themselves that in a war H-bombs would not actually be employed. They point to the fact that gas was not employed in the Second World War. I am afraid that this is a complete delusion. Gas was not employed because it was found to be indecisive and gas masks offered protection. The H-bomb, on the contrary, is a decisive weapon against which, so far, no defense has been discovered. If one side used the bomb and the other did not, the one that used it would probably reduce the other to impotence by the employment of quite a small number of bombs, such as, with any luck, would not cause much damage to the side that employed them; for the more terrible evils that are to be feared depend on the explosion of a large number of bombs. I think, therefore, that a war in which only one side employs H-bombs might end in something deserving to be called victory for that side. I do not think—and in this I am in agreement with all military authorities—that there is the slightest chance of H-bombs not being used in a world war. It follows that we must prevent large-scale wars or perish. To make the governments of the world admit this is a necessary step on the road to peace. In short, the abolition of the

H-bomb, which is a thing that we must all desire, can only come profitably after both sides have come together in a sincere attempt to put an end to the hostile relations between the two blocs. How can this be obtained?

Before any universal contracts and measures become possible two things must be achieved: first, all powerful states must realize that their aims, whatever they may be, cannot be achieved by war; second, as a consequence of the universality of this realization, the suspicion on either side that the other is preparing war must be allayed. Here are some suggestions for your consideration on the steps that can be taken to reach these two objects.

The first step should be a statement by a small number of men of the highest scientific eminence as to the effect to be expected from a nuclear war.

This statement should not suggest, however faintly, any bias in favor of either side. It is important that scientific authorities should tell us in plain language what we ought to expect in various ways, giving us definite information whenever possible, and the most likely hypothesis where conclusive evidence as yet is lacking. Most of the facts can already be ascertained, in so far as existing knowledge makes this possible, by those who are willing to take a great deal of trouble in collecting information. But what is needed is that the knowledge should be as simply stated as possible, and should be easily accessible and widely publicized, and that there should be in existence an authoritative statement to which those engaged in spreading the knowledge could appeal.

This statement would undoubtedly make clear that a nuclear war would not bring victory to either side and would not create the sort of world desired by Communists or the sort of world desired by their opponents or the sort of world that uncommitted nations desire.

Scientists throughout the world should be invited to subscribe to the technical statement and I should hope, as a further step, that this report would form a basis for action by one or more uncommitted governments. These governments could present the report, or, if they preferred it, a report drawn up by their own scientific specialists, to all the powerful governments of the world, and invite them to express their opinions upon it. The report should have such a weight of scientific authority behind it that it would be scarcely possible for any government to combat its findings. The governments on either side of the Iron Curtain could, without loss of face, simultaneously admit to uncommitted governments that war can no longer serve as a continuation of policy. Among neutrals, India is in an especially favorable position because of friendly relations with both groups as well as experience of successful mediation in Korea and Indochina. I should like to see the scientific report presented by the Indian Government to all the Great Powers with an invitation to express their opinion upon it. I should hope that all might be brought in this way to acknowledge that they have nothing to gain from a nuclear war.

Meanwhile a certain readjustment of ideas is necessary by those who have hitherto been vehement partisans of either Communism or anti-Communism. They must realize that no useful purpose is served by bitter abuse of the opposite party or by emphasis upon its past sins or by suspicions of its motives. They need not abandon their opinions as to which system would be better, any more than they need abandon their preferences in party politics at home. What all must do is to acknowledge that the propagation of the view which they prefer is to be conducted by persuasion, not by force.

Let us now assume that the Great Powers, by the methods which have been suggested, have been induced to admit that none of them could secure their aims by war. This is the most difficult step. Let us now consider what are the steps that could be taken after this initial step has been taken.

The first step, which should be taken at once, would be to secure a temporary cessation of conflict, either hot or cold, while more permanent measures were devised. Until then this temporary armistice would have to be on the basis of the *status quo* since there is no other basis that would not involve difficult negotiations. Such negotiations should follow in due course; if they are to be fruitful they must not be conducted in the atmosphere of hostility and suspicion which exists at present. During this period, when hatred and fear are abating, there should be a lessening of journalistic invective, and even well-merited criticisms of either side by the other should be muted. There should be encouragement to mutual trade and to mutual visits by deputations, especially the cultural and educational sort. All this should be by way of preparing the ground for a world conference and enabling such a conference to be more than a ruthless contest for power.

When a comparatively friendly atmosphere has been generated by these methods, a world conference should meet for the purpose of creating ways other than war by which disagreements between states should be settled. This is a stupendous task, not only through its vastness and intricacy, but also through the very real conflicts of interests that may arise. It cannot hope to succeed unless opinion has been adequately prepared. Delegates to the conference will have to meet with two firm convictions in the minds of every one of them: first, the conviction that war means total disaster; and second, the conviction that the settlement of a dispute by agreement is more advantageous to the disputants than the continuation of the dispute, even if the settlement is not wholly satisfactory to either party. If the conference is imbued with this spirit it can proceed with some hope of success to tackle the immense problems that will confront it.

The first of the problems to be tackled should be the diminution of national armaments. So long as these remain at their present level, it will be obvious that the renouncement of war is not sincere.

There should be restoration of the freedoms that existed before 1914, especially freedom of travel and freedom in the circulation of books and newspapers and the removal of obstacles to the free dissemination of ideas across national boundaries. These various restorations of former freedoms are necessary steps toward the creation of an understanding that mankind forms one family and that governmental divisions, when they become as harsh as they are at present, are difficult obstacles in the way of peace.

If these tasks were achieved, the conference would have to advance to the creation of a World Authority, already twice attempted, first by the League of Nations and then by the UN. I do not intend to go into this problem here, beyond saying that unless it is solved no other measures will have permanent value.

Ever since 1914, the world has been subject to continually deepening terror. Immense numbers of men, women and children have perished, and of the survivors a very large proportion have experienced the imminent fear of death. When people in the West think of the Russians and Chinese, and when the Russians and Chinese think of the people in the West, they think of them chiefly as a source of destruction and disaster, not as ordinary human beings with the ordinary human capacity for joy and sorrow. More and more it has come to seem as if frivolity offers the only escape from despair. The escape that can be secured by sober hope and constructive statesmanship has come to seem unobtainable. But apathetic hopelessness is not the only state of mind that is rational in the world in which we find ourselves. Almost every single person throughout the world would be happier and more prosperous if East and West gave up their quarrel. Nobody need be asked to renounce anything, unless it be the dream of world empire, which has now become far more impossible than the most wildly optimistic Utopia. We have, as never before, the means of possessing an abundance of the necessities and comforts that are needed to make life agreeable. Russia and China, if peace were secured, could devote to the production of consumer goods all the energies now devoted to rearmament. The immense scientific skill which has gone into the production of nuclear weapons could make deserts fruitful and cause rain to fall in the Sahara and Gobi deserts. With the removal of fear, new energies would spring up, the human spirit would soar and become freshly creative, and the old dark terrors that lurk in the depths of men's minds would melt away.

In a war using the H-bomb there can be no victor. We can live together or die together. I am firmly persuaded that if those of us who realize this devote ourselves with sufficient energy to the task, we can make the world realize it. Communist and anti-Communist alike prefer life to death, and if the issue is clearly presented to them, they will choose the measures which are necessary for preserving life. This is a strenuous hope, for it demands on the part of those of us who see the issue in all its jagged outline the expenditure of an immense energy in persuading, with always the difficult realization that the time is short, and with always the temptation to hysteria which comes from contemplating the possible abyss. But although the hope is arduous, it should be vivid. It should be held firmly through whatever discouragements. It should inspire the lives, first perhaps of comparatively few, but gradually of increasing numbers, until with a great shout of joy men come together to celebrate the end of organized killing and the inauguration of a happier era than any that has ever fallen to the lot of man.

ABOUT THE AUTHOR

BERTRAND ARTHUR WILLIAM RUSSELL, 3rd Earl Russell, Viscount Amberley, born in Wales, May 18, 1872. Educated at home and at Trinity College, Cambridge. During World War I, served four months in prison as a pacifist, where he wrote *Introduction to Mathematical Philosophy*. In 1910, published first volume of *Principia Mathematica* with Alfred Whitehead. Visited Russia and lectured on philosophy at the University of Peking in 1920. Returned to England and, with his wife, ran a progressive school for young children in Sussex from 1927 to 1932. Came to the United States, where he taught philosophy successively at the University of Chicago, University of California at Los Angeles, Harvard, and City College of New York. Awarded the Nobel Prize for Literature in 1950. Has been active in disarmament and anti-nuclear-testing movements while continuing to add to his large number of published books.